The SENCO Survival Guide

'**Still the best "all round" guide for SENCOs on the market,**' *Pippa Whittaker, Curriculum Leader for Inclusion, City Academy, Bristol*

The SENCO Survival Guide is an informative resource, fully updated with the new 2014 SEND Code of Practice and containing practical advice to help SENCOs manage their responsibilities and lead their school effectively towards a common goal. In light of current developments, this resource sets out the government's fresh agenda for whole school discussion and helps SENCOs in mainstream or special schools, at every stage, to manage changes in SEND policy and practice.

With up-to-date information on the changes taking place to support learners with SEN and disabilities, this fully revised new edition also includes:

- strategies to break the cycle of SEND low achievement;
- advice on crucial aspects of the SENCO role, including assessment, provision mapping, preparing for OFSTED, disability discrimination and equality;
- advice on training, managing and deploying teaching assistants effectively;
- ways in which the enhanced role of parents can be harnessed, in order to achieve maximum success for learners with SEND.

This book will give SENCOs the confidence, skills and knowledge to promote maximum achievement for learners with SEND in all schools, across all key stages and will support them in their role to develop and shape their schools' policies and practices on SEND. This book will also be of use to other members of staff looking for practical strategies to raise the attainment of all pupils with SEN and disabilities.

Sylvia Edwards is an independent SEN consultant.

Other titles published in association with the National Association for Special Educational Needs (nasen):

Language for Learning in the Secondary School: A practical guide for supporting students with speech, language and communication needs
Sue Hayden and Emma Jordan
2012/pb: 978-0-415-61975-2

Using Playful Practice to Communicate with Special Children
Margaret Corke
2012/pb: 978-0-415-68767-6

The Equality Act for Educational Professionals: A simple guide to disability and inclusion in schools
Geraldine Hills
2012/pb: 978-0-415-68768-3

More Trouble with Maths: A teacher's complete guide to identifying and diagnosing mathematical difficulties
Steve Chinn
2012/pb: 978-0-415-67013-5

Dyslexia and Inclusion: Classroom Approaches for Assessment, Teaching and Learning, 2ed
Gavin Reid
2012/pb: 978-0-415-60758-2

Promoting and Delivering School-to-School Support for Special Educational Needs: A practical guide for SENCOs
Rita Cheminais
2013/pb: 978-0-415-63370-3

Time to Talk: Implementing outstanding practice in speech, language and communication
Jean Gross
2013/pb: 978-0-415-63334-5

Curricula for Teaching Children and Young People with Severe or Profound and Multiple Learning Difficulties: Practical strategies for educational professionals
Peter Imray and Viv Hinchcliffe
2013/pb: 978-0-415-83847-4

Successfully Managing ADHD: A handbook for SENCOs and teachers
Fintan O'Regan
2014/pb: 978-0-415-59770-8

Brilliant Ideas for Using ICT in the Inclusive Classroom, 2ed
Sally McKeown and Angela McGlashon
2015/pb: 978-1-138-80902-4

Boosting Learning in the Primary Classroom: Occupational therapy strategies that really work with pupils
Sheilagh Blyth
2015/pb: 978-1-13-882678-6

Beating Bureaucracy in Special Educational Needs, 3ed
Jean Gross
2015/pb: 978-1-138-89171-5

The SENCO Survival Guide

The nuts and bolts of everything you need to know

Second edition

Sylvia Edwards

 Routledge
Taylor & Francis Group

LONDON AND NEW YORK

 nasen
Helping Everyone Achieve

Second edition published 2016
by Routledge
2 Park Square, Milton Park, Abingdon, Oxon OX14 4RN

and by Routledge
711 Third Avenue, New York, NY 10017

Routledge is an imprint of the Taylor & Francis Group, an informa business

First edition published by Routledge 2011

British Library Cataloguing in Publication Data
A catalogue record for this book is available from the British Library

Library of Congress Cataloging in Publication Data
Names: Edwards, Sylvia, author.
Title: The SENCO survival guide : the nuts and bolts of everything you need to
know / Sylvia Edwards.
Description: Second editon. | Milton Park, Abingdon, Oxon ; New York, NY :
Routledge, 2016.
Identifiers: LCCN 2015036969| ISBN 9781138931251 (hardback : alk. paper) |
ISBN 9781138931268 (pbk. : alk. paper) | ISBN 9781315679839 (ebook)
Subjects: LCSH: Learning disabilities--Great Britain. | Students with disabilities--
Education--Great Britain.
Classification: LCC LC4706.G7 E39 2016 | DDC 371.90941--dc23LC record
available at http://lccn.loc.gov/2015036969

ISBN: 978-1-138-93125-1 (hbk)
ISBN: 978 1 138 93126-8 (pbk)
ISBN: 978-1-315-67983-9 (ebk)

Typeset in Bembo
by Saxon Graphics Ltd, Derby

Printed and bound in Great Britain by
TJ International Ltd, Padstow, Cornwall

Contents

Acknowledgements

Thanks are due to colleagues in both mainstream and special schools, and in SEN services, alongside whom I have developed my ideas, knowledge and experience over many years of teaching and training others.

More recently, I would like to thank the SENCOs who have kindly shared their thoughts and issues with me, the children and young people with special educational needs and disabilities who I have tutored, and whose learning difficulties and experiences have further shaped my views on how to promote success for learners with SEND. I also wish to thank the parents of these children, with whom I have had numerous conversations, and whose views and experiences have also informed this second edition.

Introduction

Education is constantly on the move and schools are once again faced with changes in policies and practices for learners with special educational needs and disabilities (SEND). Much has moved on since the first edition of this book was published in 2011. I sincerely hope the updated content will inspire fresh reflection, and act as a mentor and guide for all Special Educational Needs Coordinators (SENCOs) in support of their quest to provide the best possible provision, leading to success for *all* learners with SEND.

Who is this book written for?

The book is written for SENCOs in mainstream or special schools, who feel they need to know more about SEND and the implications for school policy and practice, in the light of recent changes. The book will be particularly helpful for inexperienced SENCOs, helping them to respond confidently to the challenges of setting up and managing a support system that further narrows the achievement gap between SEND and non-SEND learners. For SENCOs who see their personal success reflected in the achievements of learners that are hard to teach and struggle to learn … this book is for you.

What does this book do?

The book aims to promote maximum achievement for learners with SEND in all schools across every key stage, in which the strategic role of the SENCO is pivotal. This book links together key ideas and recent developments that impact significantly on the SENCO role. The book supports SENCOs in developing the necessary personal and professional qualities, and leadership skills, that shape their school's ethos, culture, policies and practice, and conform to the Award for SEN Co-ordination (National College for Teaching and Leadership 2014).

As well as offering advice and information, the book invites reflection and debate in schools on changing policies and practices, in the light of the SEND Code of Practice and other key developments. The book will help SENCOs to reflect critically on how their particular school needs to improve, and enhance their confidence to work with other key players to develop cultural and systemic change, and ultimately, the creative solutions that will raise achievement for *all* learners with SEND.

Recent developments: Core questions

This book poses (and attempts to answer) many questions to stimulate school debate; for example:

- How has society's perception of SEN changed, and what are the implications *now*?
- How will the new Code change schools' provision for learners with SEND?
- How will the new Equality Act impact on pupils with disabilities?
- How can schools best utilise agreed models for teaching/learning to improve results?
- What is personalised learning, and why is it an essential component for SEND learners?

- Which learners are underachieving? How can schools eradicate underachievement?
- How can schools narrow the achievement gap and ensure good progress for all?
- What might assessment look like without National Curriculum levels?
- How do staff roles and responsibilities impact on SEND achievement?
- What does Quality First Teaching (QFT) look like, and how is it achieved for all learners?
- Finally, but *most* importantly, how can schools harness the enhanced roles of parents and pupils, in order to achieve maximum success for learners with SEND?

Pupil and parent power is here and is set to transform the whole balance of family and professional relationships.

There are so many questions for schools to find answers to! All schools are different, largely because staffing, learner populations and geographical location are also different.

Structure

The book reflects the Code of Practice; 'assess–plan–do–review':

- Part I identifies the needs of learners with SEND (assess);
- Part II makes appropriate provision (plan and do);
- Part III evaluates progress, using pupil and parent voices (review).

Each chapter:

- Sets out its main theme, and presents key ideas and/or principles that underpin policy;
- Explores and interrogates relevant issues;
- Offers practical help and suggestions for good practice;
- Contributes to the SENCO's effective performance.

No book offers all the answers. This guide offers a range of solutions to the problems that schools are currently grappling with, and places SENCOs firmly in the driving seat towards SEND success. Above all, the book provides SENCOs with the confidence to become movers and shakers for change. Why? Because experience has proved that whatever is happening in education today, tomorrow will always be different.

Part 1

Identifying the needs of learners with SEND

Chapter 1

Rethinking special educational needs and learning difficulties

Ever since the first realisation that children with SEN (Special Educational Needs) are *not* 'ineducable' their education has been problematic. The debate of how best to educate such a diverse group of children with difficulties in learning has raged for decades — and continues. This chapter considers:

- how perceptions of SEN have changed
- types of SEN
- what's in a label.

Outdated perceptions of SEN

There has never been a better time, especially under the new Code of Practice (DfE/DH 2015), to consider what 'SEN' means now, and what it used to mean, as outdated perceptions of children with SEN continue to limit progress. For years, the term has referred to pupils who:

- were slow learners — unlikely to meet the expectations of 'normal' peers;
- would be better educated in special schools;
- were unlikely to access a mainstream curriculum;
- should be taught by SEN specialists;
- were more likely to have a disadvantaged background.

The final point still applies today. Such views would now appear not only unthinkable but downright insulting to the parents of learners with SEN, and to learners themselves.

Rarely, in the days of 'integration', when children started to attend mainstream, did schools adapt teaching. If a child did not fit in, then it was back to the special school for many. SEN thinking has come a long way, and has now reached a further crossroads.

What has changed?

The movement from integration towards inclusion has led to further significant change. For example:

- More learners with SEN attend mainstream schools;
- All teachers are teachers of SEN. This much-rehearsed statement now has fresh implications;
- Changes to the school workforce, with increased numbers, and changed roles, for teaching assistants;
- Recognition that children with SEN **can** achieve, with appropriate support;
- Recognition that challenging behaviour is often linked to learning difficulty;
- The expectation that most children with SEN attend mainstream schools. Only those with the most severe and complex difficulties require special education;
- Increased recognition of the role of parents in education;

- Increased recognition of the role of learners with SEN in their progress and aspirations;
- Acceptance that the educational needs of learners with SEN are on an equal footing with those of all learners;
- Recognition that learning and well-being go hand in hand; that children who are unhappy, stressed or lack confidence cannot learn until their problems are dealt with.

The phrase 'for all' now carries an expectation that all children should be able to access everything and opportunities should be available for every learner.

With regard to well-being, the five outcomes in Table 1.1, that originally emerged from 'Every Child Matters' (DfES 2003a), followed by 'The Children's Plan' (DCSF 2007c), should still influence schools' approaches to success for all. The Plan set out a long-term strategy to place children and families at the heart of national and school policy-making. Most schools now have a strong commitment to placing well-being at the heart of successful learning.

Table 1.1 Every child matters: Improving outcomes for learners with Special Educational Needs and Disabilities (SEND)

Being healthy	Improved health outcomes for children and young people
Staying safe	Improved safeguarding in schools
Enjoying and achieving	Making learning fun, as well as successful and productive
Making a positive contribution	Improved participation and engagement in the local community and society
Achieving economic well-being	Able to earn a living and manage life as independently as possible

It has taken many years for some schools to make their journey from outdated to modern perceptions of children with SEN, but there is still some way to go if *all* children with SEN are to reach their potential, and experience that same sense of belonging that those without SEN enjoy.

Special educational needs and learning difficulties

What is a learning difficulty, and how does it result in a special educational need? The new Code of Practice (DfE/DH 2015) states that children have a 'special educational need if they have a learning difficulty that calls for special provision to be made....' Children have a learning difficulty if they have a 'significantly greater difficulty in learning than the majority'. The definition of 'learning difficulty' raises questions:

- How 'significantly greater' does the difficulty in learning need to be before it becomes a 'special educational need'?
- What proportion of children comprise a 'majority'?
- At what point does SEN become a disability (Chapter 3).

Who has SEN? Who does not? There are no hard and fast rules and no cut-off points. So assessing children who fall behind in learning is fraught with difficulty. When does such a fallback indicate SEN, and when does it not? The traditional acceptance that about 20% of children are likely to have some form of SEN is now open to challenge. Since 2010, the percentage of children identified with SEN has fallen to approximately 15% (DfE 2015b).

Types of SEN

Table 1.2 lists types of SEN included in the data sent by schools to inform the Government's database (DfE 2015b).

Table 1.2 SEN type data

SpLD: Specific learning difficulties
MLD: Moderate learning difficulties
SLD: Severe learning difficulties
PMLD: Profound and multiple learning difficulties
SEMH: Social, emotional and mental health problems
SLCN: Speech, language and communication needs
HI: Hearing impairment
VI: Visual impairment
MSI: Multisensory impairment
PD: Physical difficulty
ASD: Autistic spectrum disorder
OTH: Other learning difficulty or disability

Schools are required to identify a main area of need, with one other if necessary. Whilst such data informs Government statistics, how far does it help schools to provide for multi-faceted needs? Examples:

- Jeremy has ASD, with MLD and SLCN
- Tom has ADHD (attention deficit hyperactivity disorder), with ASD
- Sahir has SLD, with VI and SLCN
- Ellie has PD and VI.

These examples illustrate huge numbers of children with multi-faceted SEN, the less dominant forms of which are often submerged beneath the main difficulties, unrecognised and, therefore, not provided for.

The problems are compounded for learners whose first language is not English, although the lack of English itself is *not* a SEN. The problem for teachers and Special Educational Needs Coordinators (SENCOs) is how to identify every facet of a child's learning difficulties that forms a barrier to learning. This, in my view, is the starting point to understanding SEN.

Descriptions of SEN types

The types of SEN listed in Table 1.2 are labels … often for life! Whilst SEN labels are assigned to pupils as a way of categorising learning difficulties and organising additional support, such a label will follow a child like a shadow, throughout schooling, often into adulthood. It is then easy for schools, education/health specialists, police and society, including prospective employers, to see the label, but not the person.

Consider some of the characteristics of learners with types of SEN listed in Table 1.2.

1. *Moderate learning difficulties (MLD)*: Pupils with MLD have a generalised cognitive difficulty. Such learners may be slow to complete work, forget what they have to do, get muddled up with tasks and may always struggle to keep up with peers. Some MLD learners should achieve average expectations with appropriate support, if they have no other difficulty that impacts on learning. Most MLD learners can access the National Curriculum, though they may always need additional support to keep up. MLD is often the most common type of SEN in schools.
2. *Severe learning difficulties (SLD)*: Pupils with SLD have a more severe cognitive learning difficulty, and are more likely to have additional needs, such as SLCN. Many children with SLD can be taught to use language normally, without signing. Whilst a few SLD learners access the National Curriculum at a low level, many more work slowly through the P Scales at pre-National Curriculum levels (DfEE/ QCA 2001), mainly from Level 4 to Level 8, until they reach secondary school. It is often assumed that pupils with Down's syndrome have SLD. Some may, but amongst any group with Down's syndrome there are also 'high flyers', whose abilities deserve to be recognised.

3. *Profound and multiple learning difficulties (PMLD)*: Pupils with PMLD have the greatest degree of cognitive impairment. Many remain at P levels throughout schooling (DfEE/QCA 2001). These learners often communicate through signing and the use of IT. The majority of PMLD learners are educated in special schools because the specialist equipment that enables them to progress is not generally available in mainstream. Some PMLD pupils may be subject to rapidly changing mood swings, challenging behaviours, and are highly likely to have accompanying medical or sensory difficulties.

MLD, SLD and PMLD are types of cognitive learning difficulties along a continuum. Therefore, for each of the three categories, there are 'able and less able' at either end. Into which box does a child fit? There is such a fine line between some MLD and SLD learners that assigning a SEN label may lead towards inaccurate assumptions that work against the principle of high expectations and aspirations for all.

4. *Speech, language and communication needs (SLCN)*: These difficulties include:

    *   poor articulation of speech sounds;
    *   inadequate vocabulary that also limits reading development;
    *   poor processing of receptive language: not understanding the meaning of others;
    *   ineffective expressive language: not able to form sentences or make own meaning clear;
    *   contextual difficulties: inability to adapt language to suit different social situations.

A further complexity is whether the SLCN is caused by a delay, or a disorder that requires specialist input. Children who are delayed or disordered in terms of language experience huge difficulties across the curriculum, as speaking and listening underpin all other learning.

5. *Specific learning difficulties (SpLD)*: These include dyslexia (words), dysgraphia (writing), dyspraxia (movement) and dyscalculia (number). A pupil with dyslexia may only struggle with reading, spelling and writing. A child with dyscalculia may struggle only in Maths. A child with dyspraxia struggles with fine/gross motor coordination. Children with specific learning difficulties should achieve in all areas that are unaffected by the difficulty. Whilst specific learning difficulties are included in the Code of Practice as cognitive, they are not generalised in the way that MLD, SLD and PMLD are.
6. *Hearing or Visual impairment (HI or VI)*: Learners with sensory difficulties, but no other type of SEN, should be able to keep up with average expectations once barriers to curricular access are removed. Depending on the severity of the impairment, learners may need enlarged font, teacher radio aids, or other adaptations. The problem for schools lies in identifying other areas of SEN that sensory difficulties may obscure.
7. *Social, emotional and mental health (SEMH)*: Challenging behaviour presents more problems than any other SEN group. Yet, few pupils set out to be deliberately disruptive. Often, beneath the surface, lie associated difficulties that have led to frustration, then to behavioural difficulties; for example:

    *   Alan throws his book across the room because he can't write and feels a failure;
    *   Jenny nips other children because she can't understand what the teacher is saying and feels bored and frustrated;
    *   Bobby is disruptive in most lessons and frequently gets detention for not doing homework, mainly because he finds the tasks too challenging.

Few learners have the kind of emotional problems that do not have SEN difficulties as their source. SEMH could be reduced by addressing social, emotional and learning needs more effectively, before problems escalate and seriously affect a learner's mental health.

8. *Autistic spectrum disorder (ASD):* Autistic learners struggle with social interaction, and include high-functioning ASD (Asperger's syndrome). Learners with ASD struggle to conform to the rules and routines of school life and sometimes prefer working alone, often to their own agenda. ASD should not prevent a learner from achieving average expectations or above, but many autistic learners have other SEN problems that complicate accurate assessment and provision.
9. *Physical difficulty (PD):* The needs of learners with physical difficulties are often obvious, and so should be the solutions. Access for PD learners may be about getting between classrooms, or having desks and seating at the right height. Where there are no accompanying difficulties PD learners should achieve at least average expectations.
10. *Multisensory impairment (MSI):* MSI learners have complex difficulties, including hearing, visual and possibly other forms of SEN.
11. *Attention deficit hyperactivity disorder (ADHD):* Where do behavioural difficulties overlap into ADHD? Teachers often comment on children who cannot attend and concentrate for any length of time. Yet the majority of learners with ADHD can be trained to focus on learning activities and succeed.

So what are schools to make of categories of SEN that place children into learning boxes? How helpful are such labels for children who have more than one source of learning difficulty? In my view, not a lot. It is tempting for schools to try to teach each box of learners in a similar way, taking no account of the differences, as well as the commonalities. Do we need to look behind SEN labels?

Behind the SEN labels

What is the main purpose behind SEN diagnosis? Is it to provide the most appropriate intervention? Is it to make it easier for schools to teach children with SEN? Is the SEN label sometimes the result of parental pressure? Is it easier to diagnose SEN than to deal with aspects of underachievement differently? Maybe all of these, to some extent.

Labels may also reflect the specialist who has made an assessment. A paediatrician may diagnose ASD, whilst a speech and language therapist may diagnose the same child as having a semantic pragmatic language disorder (difficulties in the use and meaning of language). A behaviour specialist may identify strategies to address the behaviour, but the underlying cause may not be addressed at all. Once a child has been given a diagnosis by one specialist the question of any other area of difficulty may not even be posed. A diagnosis of SEN can act as a smokescreen, separating schools, parents and external professionals from the real learners behind their labels.

Raising SEN attainment

Table 1.3 (DCSF 2009a) illustrates the percentage of pupils with SEND that attained Level 4 or above in 2009. The data tells its own story of failure: not of learners, but of an education system that has allowed such underachievement to happen. Why? Because having sought to include many more children with SEND in the mainstream, schools have not been given the resources they need to rise to the inclusion challenge. In addition, for the children who have been included, their SEN label has too often been accompanied by low expectations and complacency.

What are we to deduce from Table 1.3? Is the situation suggested by these results as dire as it appears? This data assumes only one predominant area of SEN for each child, and may therefore mask other factors that could explain such poor results, including a learner's less predominant learning difficulties.

On the other hand, if children with MLD represent the largest category of SEN learners, can we really expect only about 11% to reach average levels? What about the other 89% of MLD learners? Could some of these children have achieved better, and if so, how? Can we really only expect about half of the learners with sensory difficulties to achieve the average, notwithstanding other difficulties? And what about a third of those who have physical difficulties, and also about one third with behaviour difficulties? What about

Table 1.3 Percentage of Key Stage 2 (KS2) learners with SEND achieving Level 4 or above in 2009

Type of SEND	% Level 4 or above	Type of SEND	% Level 4 or above
SpLD (specific learning difficulties)	24	VI (visual impairment)	53
MLD (moderate learning difficulties)	11	PD (physical difficulties)	34
SLD (severe learning difficulties)	2	MSI (multisensory impairment)	30
PMLD (profound and multiple learning difficulties)	1	ASD (autistic spectrum disorder)	30
BESD (behavioural, emotional and social difficulties. Now SEMH; social, emotional and mental health)	36	SLCN (speech, language and communication needs)	19
		OTHER	29
HI (hearing impairment)	42		

one quarter of those with specific learning difficulties who include children with dyslexia and dyspraxia? Is this success rate for specific learning difficulties (SpLD) realistic, or does it represent gross under-achievement?

Finally, can schools really expect pupils with SLD and PMLD to achieve Level 4, given the nature of these types of SEN as severely and profoundly cognitive? Could this small percentage of children have been significantly misdiagnosed in the first place?

Data such as this opens up many areas for debate in schools. For example:

- If these percentages of attainment *do* match their diagnoses of SEN then why did more children not achieve them?
- How accurately have all of the children represented in this data been diagnosed?

The data in Table 1.3 informs us that something was wrong somewhere!

Jumping forward, how far has the situation improved? The OFSTED report for 2013/14 (OFSTED 2014) suggests that whilst there are improvements, the achievement gap between learners with and without SEN is still not closing quickly enough, and that disadvantaged children, many of whom also have SEN, are still failed by the system. The report also suggests that primary schools are improving faster than secondary schools, and that secondaries are struggling to identify the needs of pupils accurately enough to teach the curriculum in ways that meet those needs.

Varying evidence suggests that, apart from children with the most significant learning difficulties that emerge early, low achievement escalates through greater challenges. The 2014 phonic-screening for 6 year olds, included in the OFSTED report, has revealed that whilst the results for reading and writing were 90% and 86%, respectively, only 79% of children went on to reach Level 4 at the end of Year 6. So, whilst recognising that phonics is not the only determinant of literacy achievement, we should still question what has happened in-between. Furthermore, the report reveals that the attainment gaps between SEN and non-SEN are worse for reading and writing.

Another report on trends in literacy standards states that by the end of KS2, one in five children are still not meeting expected standards in literacy (Dyslexia Action 2012). It seems that, in spite of schools' valiant efforts, supported by targeted government intervention, the oft-quoted long tail of underachievement that has cast its shadow for decades on the life chances of children with SEN, has not yet gone away.

An article in *The Times* suggests that the forty-year-old experiment to integrate children into mainstream education has caused much division and suffering; that autistic children have often been 'dismissed by teachers as difficult or lazy', and that children with SEND are still regularly bullied (Thompson 2015). The writer states a reduction in special schools of approximately 25%. Yet I cannot agree that integration has been a total failure. Schools and society are simply not there yet. And of course, mainstream education is not suitable for all. The process of inclusion still has far to go if all children are to reach their potential in either school setting. Where would the children who have been included be if they had remained in special schools *unnecessarily*? Stigmatised? Unfulfilled? Nevertheless, the inclusion process must speed up if we are to prevent further failure.

So what could be done to improve matters? Strategies could include:

- Highlighting strengths as well as weaknesses. Dual exceptionality may mean that SEN in one area is balanced by a special talent in another;
- Drilling down to identify and address all learners' weaknesses and unique needs;
- Not identifying SEN before all other strategies have been tried;
- Reaching behind the façade of SEMH to identify possible SEN;
- Placing self-esteem at the heart of teaching and learning;
- Knowing each learner! Which ones CAN achieve average expectations once barriers to learning are removed?
- Policies that are flexible enough to meet a diverse range of needs; for example, a one-size-fits-all policy for behaviour cannot work for all learners with SEMH;
- Setting high (but realistic) expectations and aspirations for all learners, based on prior attainment and achievement. The 'I can' approach enables all learners to succeed.

Finally, Dyson (2015) identifies three areas where SEN has become problematic, and in which assumptions need to be further challenged. These are:

- *Boys*: given that about three times more boys than girls are identified with SEN, what is it about 'boyness' that presents a problem?
- *Family income*: why is it that the poorer a child is, the more likely that the child will be identified with SEN?
- *Ethnicity and culture*: there is no reason why the percentage of ethnic groups identified with SEN should be higher than the rest of the school population (travellers are four times more likely).

Dyson therefore concludes that too many children are still being identified with SEN, not because of their individual differences, but on a *social* basis. SENCOs need to question whether these trends apply to their own SEN cohorts as there is no 'cure' for maleness, ethnicity and disadvantage. Perhaps these trends need to be attacked from an alternative perspective, following the question of whether SEN diagnoses arise as much from social and organisational factors as from innate individual differences. In my view, only significant cognitive learning difficulties can provide justifiable reasons for low achievement.

Chapter summary

This chapter may have generated more questions than answers for SENCOs. Could the way through this maze of labels and coexisting areas of difficulty be to focus on needs, and cease to bother about which SEN category children fall into? Should schools concentrate mainly on what children find difficult about learning? Would dispensing with SEN labels help schools and external specialists to devise joint strategies to remove barriers and guarantee more success for SEN learners? Maybe.

On the other hand, whilst the Government continues to convert SEN labels into statistics, it appears unlikely that schools can ever dispense with them. Schools can, however, do two things:

- Challenge the false assumptions (gender, social, ethnic) through which SEN labels often emerge;
- Refuse to allow SEN labels to smother the high expectations that drive teaching and learning for all.

'Excellence and Enjoyment: A Strategy for Primary Schools' (DfES 2003b) summarised the common aim that, 'Our education system must not write off any child through low expectations', and reminded us that 'children learn better when they are excited and engaged ... through excellent teaching', which 'challenges them and shows them what they can do'. That same message applies today.

The big questions for SENCOs are: Which learners with SEND could do better? And, how can our school make it happen?

The rest of this book highlights issues for SENCOs to reflect upon, with practical strategies towards breaking the cycle of low achievement and closing the unacceptable gap between SEND and non-SEND.

Chapter 2

The new Code

From labels to needs

Chapter 1 explored traditional and newly evolved concepts of special educational needs, and invited SENCOs to think about the implications for learners with 'SEN' labels. This chapter moves from labels to needs and considers:

- The new SEN Code of Practice: a graduated response;
- The four areas of need for learners with SEN;
- Working with external specialists;
- Assessment at local authority (LA) level, from statements to Education, Health and Care Plans (EHCPs);
- Flexibility, challenge and personalisation: ways forward.

Having regard for the Code

Since 1994, when the first Code of Practice for SEN came into effect, schools have been required to 'have regard'. The Codes have set out duties for Local Authorities, schools and other professionals to identify, assess and make provision for children with SEN. The revised Code (DfE/DH 2015) now reflects the Children and Families Act (DfE 2014a), and remains the foundation of the SEN system. So, what has changed?

- Extended age range, from 0 to 25;
- Further includes disability with SEN;
- Stronger focus on high aspirations and outcomes for children and young people;
- Better joint planning/commissioning: education, health and social care working together;
- A local offer of services for pupils with SEND;
- New guidance on the graduated approach to managing SEN, merging School Action and School Action Plus;
- A coordinated assessment process at LA level replaces statements with Education, Health and Care Plans (EHCP);
- Greater focus on enabling all children with SEN to achieve and make a successful transition into adulthood.

Transitional arrangements are in place for schools and LAs to move *strategically* to the new system. It is expected that all children with a statement will have an EHCP, as the legal test remains the same.

The definitions of learning difficulty and SEN are mostly unchanged. The implications from the new Code are for a more rigorous approach to assessing and providing for children with SEND. Advice on the Code states that a child or young person:

- Has SEN … if they have a learning difficulty or disability which calls for special educational provision to be made;

- Has a disability that prevents ... from making use of facilities of a kind generally provided for others of the same age in mainstream schools;
- Educational provision is described as 'education or training ... additional to or different from that made generally for others ...

(DfE/DH 2015, p.16)

There are stronger references to disability from the Equality Act (DfE 2014b), a more flexible approach between mainstream and special education, and stronger duties to fully involve parents at every stage of the graduated response. OFSTED will look closely at how schools' policies and practices reflect the new Code.

From labels to needs

The new Code continues to offer a description of learning difficulties that helps schools to make accurate assessments and appropriate provision for children with SEND, and also invites schools to take an overview of learners' needs and consider 'what action ... to take', and in particular, to 'not fit a pupil into a category [of SEN]' (DfE/DH 2015, section 6.27).

Reflecting on categories of SEN in terms of *needs* invites schools to delve more deeply into each 'SEN box', as well as inviting teachers to look closely at their learning environment, in order to match classroom activities more closely to individual learner's needs.

Table 2.1 lists the Code's four broad areas of need with examples of *likely* SEN categories. Medical needs are not included here, but some learners with SEND have medical problems that add further complexity to their learning or physical needs.

Table 2.1 illustrates how the four broad areas of need are likely to overlap with SEN types. Cognition and learning subsumes four types, and includes specific learning difficulties with those that are generalised. Communication and interaction includes children with SLCN and ASD, and social, educational and mental health needs cover a huge range of SEN areas. Sensory and physical needs may also overlap into the other three areas.

This reflection on labels versus areas of need invites SENCOs to rethink two key aspects of their role:

- Supporting quality first teaching in classrooms (QFT);
- Managing the SEND whole-school system.

Let's focus firstly on how broad areas of need affect classrooms. The Code specifies that special educational provision must be matched with high-quality teaching that is differentiated to meet individual pupil's needs. Imagine a classroom with:

- 1 pupil with ASD
- 3 pupils with significant literacy difficulties (including dyslexia)
- 2 pupils with behavioural difficulties
- 3 pupils with some cognitive learning difficulties
- 1 pupil with a visual impairment.

Table 2.1 Broad areas of need and likely SEN types

Broad areas of need	Types of SEN most likely to apply
Communication and interaction	ASD, SLCN, SEMH, SLD, PMLD
Cognition and learning	PMLD, SLD, MLD — generalised, SpLD — specific
Social, emotional and mental health	SEMH, ASD, SLCN (social)
Sensory and/or physical	HI, VI, PD, PMLD

We might also imagine that, of these ten learners, six represent the typical percentage of SEN and the other four represent children who struggle to keep up *without* a SEN diagnosis. For any teacher, organising learning around these different needs, with due regard for the needs of learners without difficulties, is an awesome task. No wonder teaching is such a stressful job. Both challenges and solutions depend as much on teaching styles as on learning styles. Clusters of schools could work together to find solutions, starting from the broad areas of need. The fact that there are no firm cut-off points for a diagnosis of SEN strengthens the case for broad areas of need as the way forward.

Is classroom planning easier for teachers and more effective for learners by focusing most academic lessons on broad areas of need? Furthermore, could these four areas act as planning templates from which to generate workable solutions for teachers and SENCOs? If so, how might it work?

Table 2.2 offers a starting point for thinking about learners' needs and whole-class lessons. Communication and interaction difficulties affect language and the social structure of tasks and activities. Cognition and learning adaptations take place mainly during the 'doing' part of the lesson, as differentiated activities along the same theme: for example, in a lesson on equivalent fractions some pupils would have much simpler fraction challenges. Social, emotional and mental health needs can ruin the most well-planned lesson, so strategies would be built into each part. Sensory and physical adaptations may also need to be stretched throughout every part of the lesson.

Table 2.2 Planning from four broad areas of need

Lesson	Communication and interaction	Cognition and learning	Social, emotional and mental health	Sensory and physical
Introduction	Adapting language and instructions	Stepped instructions	Behaviour strategies Rewards Sanctions	Seating Position in class Visual aids Hearing aids
Tasks/activities and resources	Working alone, as pairs or in groups	Backtracking: different levels of challenge	Same	Same
Close	Language and instructions	Summarise learning	Same	Same

How might such planning work for the imagined class referred to above? Table 2.3 matches these learners to the broad areas of need most likely to be revealed. Of course it is not as simple as this, but Table 2.3 illustrates how SEND and non-SEND difficulties can be accommodated together, and offers a template to generate the detailed discussions that only teachers and SENCOs can have, concerning their particular school with its unique learner population.

Such juggling reminds us that teachers are managers, both of learning and of children or young people. Table 2.3 also illustrates how children with SEN may present more than one broad area of need. In any

Table 2.3 Matching SEND and non-SEND difficulties with areas of need

Area: Pupils	Communication and interaction	Cognition and learning	Social, emotional and mental health	Sensory and physical
SEND difficulties	Jamie: ASD	Jamie: ASD Alice: dyslexia Nathan: MLD	Jamie: ASD Tom: SEMH	Helen: VI
Non-SEND difficulties Lesson Introduction Main part Close	Seema: language Abdul: language	John: phonics	Elise: disruptive	

typical class, teachers must *know* the children they teach, and also know how their combined learning needs are spread across the four broad areas.

Changes to the Code's graduated response

The new Code has made changes to how SENCOs need to manage their school's graduated response to children who fall behind age-related expectations. These include:

- School Action and School Action Plus, now merged into SEN Support;
- Statements in the process of becoming Education, Health and Care Plans (EHCPs);
- Funding.

Although the Code has merged the two previous in-school responses into a single category (SEN Support), the children in this category still need a graduated response. Consider the stages of response in the following subsections.

Response 1: Targeted classroom intervention

The Code stresses that the first response to children who make less-than-expected progress is 'high-quality teaching ... *targeted* at areas of weakness' (DfE/DH 2015, 6.19). Schools are advised to take particular care *not* to label a child with SEN simply because of inadequate spoken language (social or ethnic). Short-term strategies need to be tried first as temporary blips, caused by such factors as bullying, bereavement, or behaviours that stem from disadvantage, can all cause progress to falter. Sensitive solutions to short-term problems often rule out the presence of SEN.

The onus is on teachers and teaching assistants (TAs) to monitor children who become a cause for concern, may be withdrawn, are behaving differently or are not even attending school as regularly as usual. Parents should be involved in this initial problem-solving and all concerns need to be taken seriously until the possibility of SEN can be either eliminated, or confirmed.

Response 2: SEN Support

If progress remains slower than expected, despite *targeted* intervention, evidence needs to be gathered by the teacher and SENCO to see if the child may have SEN, such as:

- Samples of work: writing, spelling, maths
- Reading records and notes
- Observations of work habits and behaviour
- Teacher's marking records
- TA's notes and observations
- Observations of parents.

Such evidence should be compared with national expectations to determine the achievement gap. At this point, parents *must* be involved and invited to contribute to the evidence-gathering.

It may then be decided to place the child on SEN Support. If so:

- Parents must be formally notified that the child is at a SEN stage of intervention;
- The child should have a personal plan drawn up by the SENCO, class teacher, child and parents.

The Code no longer specifies the need for an old-style Individual Education Plan. It is up to schools to 'determine ... their own approach to record keeping' (DfE/DH 2015, 6.72). The plan needs to record accurately whatever additional provision the child receives through SEN Support, and be kept up to date. Personal plans should be:

- SMART (see following section)
- Reviewed termly, with all relevant professionals, parents and child.

Personal plans

What purpose does a personal plan have, and what should it look like? Table 2.4 expands on what constitutes a SMART (specific, manageable, achievable, relevant, timed) plan. It is for schools to decide on the format.

Both parents and learners should be fully involved in the personal plan. I have come across countless plans that have not been understood by parents or the child, the outcome being that neither has been involved in ensuring its success. Under the new arrangements, parents and learners must be involved in drawing up the personal plan and working with schools throughout its timescale, to ensure the purpose of the plan is fully achieved.

So what could be improved in personal plans? My observations, gleaned from training schools in SEN, have often been that:

- Some targets are neither specific nor measurable: '*to improve reading, to understand addition, to behave better in class or to work with others*' would be better written specifically as '*to read stories with a reading age of …, to add numbers up to a total of 20, to complete tasks without disruption, or to discuss … for 10 minutes with one peer*'. Targets need to be measured.
- Challenges have been either too easy or too hard. If challenges are too easy, learning is minimal; if too hard, the child fails to meet them.
- Social, communication and self-help targets have often been neglected, as if schools have assumed that the plan must always feature Maths and English. This is not so. The targets represent stepping stones towards achievement, so if social, communication or behavioural skills are acting as barriers to other learning, these must be *prioritised* first. The plan is *personal* to each individual learner.

At this first (mild) stage of SEN Support, children may have common needs that can be accommodated on a group plan (GP). A group plan may make it easier to manage children at this level of SEN Support, at which much of the intervention is delivered in groups (as in previous School Action). GPs may make it easier for TAs to manage interventions, but confidentiality then becomes an issue to be dealt with at reviews. GPs are only suitable for children whose needs are *common to others in the group*. Some schools may organise provision through a mix of group plans (GPs) and personal plans (PPs), thereby balancing both common and individual needs at this first 'SEN Support' stage.

Table 2.4 SMART targets for personal plans

Specific	Achievements written as targets: these should be clear, precise and understood by parents and child.
Measurable	How do we know when the child has achieved them? Can targets be observed or tested in order to measure progress from 'before to after' intervention?
Achievable	Do the targets represent reasonable levels of challenge for the child: neither too high nor too low, but comfortable, to inspire confidence and motivation?
Relevant	Do targets reflect the child's real priorities as barriers to achievement? Are they the most important skills for the child to focus on during this current timescale?
Timed	The agreed date by which the targets are expected to be achieved.

The termly review

The purpose of the review at Response 2 (previously School Action) is to summarise progress and decide whether the child:

- Has made such good progress that additional provision is no longer needed, in which case the child continues with appropriate differentiation in class, still targeted towards known weaknesses, as for Response 1;
- Has made some progress, but it is agreed that the Response 2 plan should be continued into a further term, with the same targets, or fresh ones;
- Has made very little progress and therefore should be moved to Response 3 (previously School Action Plus), with the involvement of an external specialist.

These are difficult decisions. How do schools decide what is good or less-than-expected progress for each individual learner? The Code suggests that schools might question personal progress that:

- Is significantly slower than that of the child's peer group, when all are starting from the same baseline;
- Fails to match or better previous individual rate of progress;
- Fails to close the attainment gap between the child and their peers;
- Widens the attainment gap.

These represent loose criteria that a school can build into their own policies to determine differing levels of SEN.

Who should attend termly reviews? Ideally, all the professionals involved, as well as the child and parents. Parents cannot be expected to play a full part unless they are fully involved, so the importance should be made clear as soon as a child reaches this response stage. The Code also stipulates that schools should allow time to review and plan effectively.

If there is one thing I would urge schools to do, it is to encourage all learners (where maturity allows), as well as parents, to attend reviews. Their presence often uses more valuable SENCO time, but all learners need to take partial responsibility for success: both the plan and the review are *personal only to them*. Many personal plans fail to become *personal* at all. They remain limited to school involvement, excluding the most important *person*; like a Polo mint without a centre.

At this stage, well-devised targets and effective strategies should be enough to place many children back onto their achievement track. What about the rest, whose progress remains minimal?

Response 3: SEN Support involving external specialists

Where progress has been minimal, despite Response 2 intervention having been in place for a reasonable time and fully evaluated, it might be assumed that the child has a significant learning difficulty that requires an external specialist. The Code also refers to children at the Early Years Foundation Stage (EYFS), who have made 'less-than-expected progress despite evidence-based support' as being in this more needy group (DfE/DH 2015, 5.48).

By this stage there should be much information about rates of progress and learning styles, as well as possible reasons for weaknesses that have not so far responded to the targeted intervention. Aside from known sensory or physical difficulties, are there outstanding problems in communication and interaction, cognition and learning, social skills or behaviour? Does one area stand out, or are the problems more complex?

The merging of School Action and School Action Plus into SEN Support must not blind schools to huge differences in achievement between the majority of struggling learners, whose needs *can* be met without external specialist intervention, and the minority whose needs cannot. The 'plus' element of the Code's response still applies in practice.

Once external specialists become involved, the local offer becomes highly relevant. Local Authorities have a duty to publish available support, inside and outside the local area. SENCOs need to translate the LA offer into a 'school-specific' version that is also available for parents.

Working with external specialists

So what happens now for the small proportion of children who move on to Response 3?

SENCOs need to know how each specialist service operates, and know enough about the child to select the relevant ones; for example: Education Psychologist; Speech and Language Therapist; Occupational Therapist; Learning Support or Behaviour Service.

Specialist services support schools at different levels — school, class, individual, or a combination — as illustrated in Table 2.5. How does a SENCO decide on the priorities in order to use funding wisely?

External specialist support often spreads beyond its immediate purpose. A School Improvement Service is primarily concerned with school policy and practice. The Speech and Language Therapist may initially focus on the individual, but the benefits may extend, through improved teaching, to other children in the class. A consultant from a SEN or Behaviour Support Service may initially assess individuals, but the recommendations may apply more broadly. Educational Psychologists are regularly consulted on behaviour, but their advice may spill over to class or school level.

The personal plans and termly reviews for children at Response 3 now have an added dimension — the external specialist — whose assessment and advice help to determine the next steps. Parental permission *must* be sought before a named child can be referred to an external specialist. SENCOs need to have clear criteria for referral and be able to justify the funding used for this purpose to OFSTED, governors and parents.

The review, following intervention at Response 3, may have the following outcomes:

- The child has made such good progress that an external specialist is no longer needed, in which case intervention is returned to previous levels;
- The child is still struggling to achieve, so the involvement of the specialist is continued for a further term, with more advice on targets and strategies to address the difficulties;
- The child has made such poor progress over one or more terms that a request for Local Authority assessment is agreed between the school, external specialist and parents.

This graduated response should ensure that, apart from learners with sensory or physical difficulties, only a tiny minority of children, with the most severe levels of learning difficulty, need to progress to Response 4. For many years this percentage has hovered at around 2% of the total school population.

Table 2.5 Working with external specialists

Specialist level of involvement	Examples
Individual pupils	Pupil assessments and reports
	Observing behaviour in class
	Counselling to boost self-esteem
	Working alongside pupils in class
Year group or class	Observing the learning environment
	Problem-solving at class level
	Training for staff in a particular year group
Whole school	Policy discussions
	Improvements in SEN management system
	Training on areas of SEN
	Provision mapping

Response 4: From statement to EHCP

Statements were never intended as prizes. Yet many parents have battled for a statement, as if the SEN graduated system has represented a direction of travel, with a statement as the ultimate destination. Now that statements have been replaced (process to be completed by 2017) by Education, Health and Care Plans (EHCPs), it is time for schools, and especially parents, to reflect on the types of difficulties that require an EHCP. Table 2.6 highlights differences between statements and EHCPs, adapted from a recent pathfinder research report (Spivack *et al.* 2014).

The research poses many questions for LAs and SENCOs in ensuring that the practical application of EHCPs match their expressed purpose and points out the challenges of:

- Consistency: how can different agencies work together?
- Delivering a more family centred process;
- Meeting a twenty-week time frame;
- Sharing information between agencies and families;
- Increased paperwork;
- Providing a comprehensive and integrated (all services) personal budget offer;
- Ensuring that families are enabled to engage fully with the process;
- Negotiating in family conflicts.

The family centred ways of working should lead to better quality plans that are more effective than the statements they replace. However, the same research also suggests that now is the time to improve non-statutory provision, so that fewer learners will go on to require an EHCP. A further challenge for SENCOs?

The Lamb Inquiry highlighted the dissatisfaction of parents with the statement system (DCSF 2009e). The EHCP therefore seeks to make assessment and provision simpler; a one-stop shop, involving multiple collaboration of professionals into a combined, therefore less stressful experience for parents and learners, along the principle of 'tell us once'. Parents now have greater control over EHCP outcomes. The Code points out that LAs should not 'apply a blanket policy to particular groups or types of need' (DfE/DH 2015, 9.16), reinforcing the need for personalisation to take priority over SEN labels.

For pupils with very severe levels of learning difficulty, the need may be so obvious that they need to be 'fast-tracked' towards an EHCP, and their needs met from the Early Years Foundation Stage.

Apart from those learners whose needs are obvious and urgent from an early age, or who follow changes in health or social circumstances, only a tiny minority of learners will emerge with needs that require support over and above that for which schools are solely responsible (SEN Support).

Table 2.6 Differences between statements and EHCPs

Process	Statements	EHCP
Referral for assessment	Standard information: mainly SEN focused	More emphasis on gathering information from across services to inform decision
Coordinated assessment	Parents could be involved via written input; less opportunity to meet SEN caseworkers	More family centred, integrated; includes face-to-face discussions with EHCP coordinator
Planning	Parents sent draft for review, often based on set number of hours of adult support	Family centred, high aspirations, coproduced outcomes, flexible
Cultural spirit and intention	Mainly fitted into set levels and types of SEN provision	Reduced duplication Less bureaucracy Improving communication with parents and learners A single pathway to age 25 More holistic process Collaborative decision-making

Anyone can bring a child's needs to the attention of the LA, but for this tiny minority whose needs have emerged gradually, the LA will need to be satisfied that the Code's graduated response has been followed properly, in order to merit formal assessment.

What types of evidence support the LA decision? These should include:

- Appropriate classroom differentiation: QFT;
- Well-targeted differentiation at Response 1, prior to SEN Support;
- Appropriate intervention at Response 2; SEN Support without an external specialist;
- Appropriate intervention at Response 3; SEN Support plus an external specialist.

Such evidence should show that in spite of a cumulative process of intervention, the child has still failed to progress according to any of the criteria identified above, and that the gap between the child and their peers has widened significantly.

This widening of the attainment gap may be shown by:

- Academic attainment: little or no progress;
- Progress that is significantly slow despite 'much additional intervention' over and above that usually provided (DfE/DH 2015, 9.14);
- Standardised test results that are unusually low.

The LA will also require evidence of any significant physical, health or social care needs.

The Code also reminds schools that an EHCP may be needed to ensure support into Further Education (DfE/DH 2015, 9.15). If the LA does not agree to assess or allocate an EHCP parents should be advised how to appeal.

How should schools respond to a new EHCP? Firstly, a meeting should be held to determine how best to translate the EHCP into a practical, personalised intervention that will enable it to be fully effective. This meeting should be attended by:

- All relevant school staff: SENCO, teachers and teaching assistants
- External specialists
- Parents/carers
- The child or young person.

The EHCP is considerably more complex than a statement, combining education, health and social care into a single document, and seeking an outcome for parents that is centred on the needs of the child or young person. Table 2.7 illustrates how the combined intervention of all services might be written into an EHCP. For a young person in Year 9 or beyond, the EHCP must include provision required to support adulthood. The plan is anticipatory and futuristic, reflecting a vision of success for the young person at its heart.

The choice of school for children with severe levels of SEND has long been an issue for parents. The Code reminds us that a mainstream school cannot refuse to admit a child with an EHCP unless it is 'incompatible with the efficient education of others', and that 'no reasonable steps can be taken to prevent the incompatibility' (DfE/DH 2015, 9.89). In practice, such incompatibility would be rare, as reasonable steps can almost always be made. The aspirations and needs of the child should govern the choice. Academies are covered by the same statutory requirements as maintained schools.

At the first meeting following the allocation of an EHCP, the task is to decide how it will be addressed. How do education, health and social-care needs break down into practical solutions, especially if all three areas are a vital part of the child's needs? This is problem-solving at its most complex, involving everyone who has contributed to the EHCP.

Table 2.7 Education, Health and Care Plan (EHCP)

Section Heading	Notes
A. Views, interests and aspirations	Aspirations should represent a long-term vision of the child as an adult. It may be in the form of 'About Me', written in 1st or 3rd person.
B. Description of SEN	Types of SEN and the broad areas of need that relate to the SEN should be included.
C. Health needs related to SEN or disability	These need to be specific and comprehensive; for example, any special dentistry.
D. Social-care needs related to SEN or disability	Must include assessment of social-care needs that reflect the 'Working together to Safeguard Children Act' (DfE 2015c)
E. Outcomes sought for adult life, plus arrangements for setting shorter-term targets	How will short-term targets build into the best possible outcomes that move in the direction of the young person's aspirations?
F. SEN provision required	Description of what will be provided by the EHCP from education. If needed it should be included, without recourse to cost or inconvenience. May include therapies (speech and language, physiotherapy, occupational, Child and Adolescent Mental Health Service – CAMHS). All types of training needs.
G. Health provision required	Description of what will be provided by the EHCP to meet health needs. Some therapies can appear under education or health. If Year 9, this includes preparation for adulthood.
H1. Social-care needs under the Chronically Sick and Disabled Act 1970	These refer to very significant needs that demand immediate response.
H2. Other social-care needs under the Social Care Act 2014	Other social-care provision that has resulted in the child having SEN; what is reasonably required.
I. Name/type of school that child will attend	Included only in the final plan; may be one type of school, or dual placement between special and mainstream. Education Otherwise is also included in this section.
J. Personal budget (if applicable)	Details of the budget provided to facilitate the success of the EHCP; must be enough to secure the provision specified.
K. List of information and advice gathered for the EHCP	Evidence that has contributed to the judgement: who gave it, and when.

On the education side, a priority is to break down aspirations and outcomes into short-term targets, as illustrated in Table 2.8. Opinions will differ, but learners and parents must be fully involved. Success depends on how schools, learners and parents together move the EHCP through manageable operational stages.

Parents should be helped to understand how termly targets feed into annual outcomes, and how annual outcomes follow the child's aspirations. Of course, these aspirations may change as the EHCP progresses. The aspirations shown in Table 2.8 are not that different from those of other children, yet why should they be? It may take more years for a child with an EHCP to achieve the aspirations they set out with, but they are there to guide and motivate, regardless of whether some are achieved by the age of 16, 25, or later.

A child with an EHCP in Year 3 will have changed considerably by the time that young person leaves school, following about eight annual reviews and up to twenty-four termly reviews. Throughout this timescale, schools and parents must observe carefully whether the initial aspirations have been set too high or too low, so that the EHCP can be adapted to match the growing learner, and assist that person into successful post-school support. The EHCP can only be amended following the views of parents.

How do aspirations differ from outcomes? The Code states that outcomes represent the 'benefit or difference made to an individual as a result of intervention' (DfE/DH 2015, 9.66). Outcomes are not descriptions; they are the end result. Furthermore, an outcome is 'achieved by each phase or stage', referring to termly targets. The outcomes and targets in Table 2.8 are examples. Only schools and parents know learners well enough to judge the lengths of stride each learner can make from term to term, and from year to year, towards their future aspirations.

Table 2.8 From broad aspirations to specific targets

Aspirations	Outcomes	Targets
To communicate effectively with different people	Use language to express own needs and problems Join in paired tasks	Ask adult for help if stuck Place objects in position (in, on, under) as instructed Use colour, size, shape to describe objects
To gain information from, and enjoy, reading	Read all tricky words Decode regular single-syllable words Develop vocabulary for reading Understand what is read	Recognise the first set of tricky words in books Read short words with vowel digraphs (ee, ea, oo) Answer questions at literal level from what is read
To lead an independent life, with minimal support	Deal with personal needs Gain awareness of danger Know when help is required	Deal with toilet needs alone Cross road to go to shop Ask adults for words that are not understood
To become a responsible citizen and enjoy work	Work alongside others Manage time commitments Respect the routines of school and work experience	Join in small group work Read time to the half hour Work quietly for 10-minute time span Place finished work in tray
To write basic texts: letters, emails	Spell to a simple level Write simple sentences with punctuation Know how different types of texts are set out	Spell all tricky words Use templates to produce sentences Use models to help with own writing
To manage own finances with minimal support	Understand numbers to 1,000, plus add, subtract, multiply, divide Know all notes and coins Go shopping Check own change	Add numbers to 20 Know coins up to 50p Spend coins in school shop and check change

Coordinating annual and termly reviews

Termly reviews for children with an EHCP follow a similar pattern to those described earlier, using evidence from all staff, external specialists, parents and, especially, the learners themselves. The review must revolve around the child or young person and parents. To keep everyone on track, the Code suggests that schools append documents and personal plans from termly reviews to the EHCP, to reflect the child's long-term aspirational journey.

The purpose of the annual review (at least six monthly for EYFS) is to assess the yearly outcomes on the EHCP. Have they been achieved? If so, which new outcomes will lead the learner further along their aspirational road? If termly reviews have been effective they should feed neatly into the annual review, with information already there and no big surprises. Regular checks on the direction of travel — from targets to outcomes to aspirations — will have helped to keep everyone well-focused. The EHCP review must be centred around the young person, who may require an advocate.

Transition planning must also be built into the EHCP. The annual review must be held early enough for the learner and all adults to manage the transition effectively (Code recommends February in the year of transfer). If LA reassessment of the learner is requested, it should follow the same process as for initial assessment. Similarly, any amendments to EHCPs follow the same process. The EHCP may cease if all, including parents, agree that it is no longer necessary.

A personal budget can be requested for a young person with an EHCP, but this is not an entitlement. If granted, the personal budget should clearly reflect the aspirations and intended outcomes of the EHCP, and be firmly coordinated with its education, health and social-care elements. The effectiveness of the personal budget, where applicable, should also form part of the annual review. Advice for Local Authorities and schools is available (DfE 2014e).

Flexibility, challenge and personalisation

This chapter has considered the Code's graduated response to SEN as stages that children may progress through on the way to having their personal needs fully met by the *system*. As part of the graduated response system we have also considered:

- Categories of SEN as labels
- SEN broad areas of need.

Yet, the achievement gap between SEN and non-SEN proves that systems alone are not enough. Why? Because systems are neither flexible nor uniquely personal. They ignore key differences in personality and characteristics that can mark the difference between success and failure. The diverse personalities of children with SEN may be quirky, alternative and 'out of the box', but I believe they hold the key to closing that stubborn achievement gap.

How does personalisation work? Learning for most pupils combines explicit with implicit experiences, especially in self-help and social contexts. For children without SEN much of this type of learning is implicit, absorbed from environmental experience. For children with SEN, especially those with more significant difficulties, learning may need to be more explicit. For example, most children learn to wait in the lunch queue by watching others, but a child with autism may need to be taught explicitly how to queue. Similarly, to 'work without an adult for five minutes' is not something most children need as a target, but a child with ADHD may need explicit focus on this learning skill.

These types of targets can make a huge difference to the achievement of learners with SEN, referred to in the Code as 'additional to and different from' (ATDF) what is delivered normally through the curriculum (DfE/DH 2015, 6.76). Table 2.9 illustrates how ATDF targets might be generated from diverse needs. Many individual education plans have neglected ATDF areas of need, such as self-help, independence or social skills, yet these highly personalised areas often act as barriers to learning and, where applicable, need to be *prioritised* on personal plans.

ATDF targets also demand flexibility. In order to firstly gain, and then keep their motivation, such learners need to know that schools are willing to bend in their direction some of the time. Two-way flexibility is a crucial part of the process that separates past integration from present-day inclusion. The Code also reassures schools that high-quality teaching that is differentiated and personalised works effectively for the majority. Only a few learners need ATDF approaches.

Table 2.9 Linking SEN with 'additional to and different from' (ATDF)

Type of SEN	Broad areas of need	Targets that are 'additional to and different from' (ATDF)
ASD	Communication and interaction	• to wait in the lunch queue • to relate weekend news to one peer • to put up hand and wait for adult to respond
ADHD	Communication and interaction Social, emotional and mental health	• to focus independently on a task for 5 minutes • to complete 10 sums by self
Dyslexia	Cognitive learning difficulties	• to select appropriate writing scaffold • to build spellings from known syllables • to recognise personal spelling needs
SEMH	Social, emotional and mental health	• to manage anger through agreed strategies • to use 'time out' card as appropriate
SLD	Cognitive learning difficulties	• to move around different classrooms independently • to write a simple sentence from a model • to ask for help when needed
SLCN	Communication and interaction	• to describe objects using size and colour • to ask questions in class

The third part of this section is about challenge. Consider three levels:

- Historical: Too easy. The pupil achieves the targets but has not learned anything new. Historical targets represent 'stand still'. Easy targets are only appropriate as a temporary measure, to nurture a learner's confidence, prior to gradually raising the bar.
- Challenging: Just right. Enough challenge for the learner to reach up and touch success with a reasonable amount of independence, showing steady progression.
- Idealistic: Too high to reach without support from adults. Idealistic targets nurture self-perceived failure and impact negatively on personal plans if a child has to repeat them.

This chapter has focused on learners with SEN, in terms of who they are and what their needs are, because unless schools know particular learners — forwards, backwards and upside down — teaching is unlikely to result in learning.

The Code's graduated responses may be thought of as mild, moderate or severe. SEN Support at Response 2, mainly group intervention, perhaps with a group education plan, is at a comparatively mild stage. Some of these children will improve, while others will go further into the SEN Support stage, at Response 3, with more individual support. These children have learning difficulties that are more moderate, needing the support of external specialists. The tiny proportion who need more, at Response 4, have severe needs that may result in an EHCP.

Managing the Code's graduated response

Managing the Code's graduated response is a key part of the SENCO role. Where tasks exceed time, it follows that the system must be practical and efficient, with contributions from colleagues, facilitated by effective provision-mapping and intervention arrangements.

The Code states that SENCOs should be aware of the local offer and work with other professionals, providing a support role to families, and ensuring that pupils with SEN receive appropriate support and high-quality teaching (DfE/DH 2015, 6.89).

The Code (DfE/DH 2015, 6.90) lists key responsibilities as follows:

- To manage the operation of SEN policy;
- To coordinate additional SEN provision;
- To liaise on behalf of vulnerable pupils, who also have SEN;
- Advise teachers on the Code's graduated response;
- Advise on the deployment of the delegated budget and other resources;
- Liaise with parents/carers of pupils with SEN;
- Liaise with early years (EY) providers, other schools, external specialists, health/social care;
- Be a point of contact between the school and Local Authority on support services;
- Liaise with follow-on providers about options, ensure smooth transition arrangements;
- Work with governors/head teacher to ensure the school complies with the Equality Act;
- Ensure that SEN records are up to date;
- Guide colleagues.

Tasks such as *managing, advising, coordinating* and *ensuring* can only be done by a person with management status, especially in larger schools. The Code states that SENCOs should be part of the senior leadership team and have time and resources to perform the role effectively. Table 2.10 offers a checklist that SENCOs might use to support policy-making, in collaboration with colleagues, parents and learners.

Table 2.10 Checklist for whole-school policy response to the Code

For Response 1:

- Once a child falls behind, who is involved in the initial targeted intervention? Class teachers? Subject teachers at secondary? Teaching assistants?
- How are these members of staff supported, and what role does the SENCO play?
- How is this initial response recorded, and by whom?
- Who is responsible for the records? Where are they kept? Who has a copy?

For Response 2:

- What are the criteria for placing children on SEN Support?
- How are children with disabilities linked to SEN Support?
- Where does the evidence come from, and what should it comprise?
- Who collates the evidence?
- How are the children recorded: using SEN type, broad areas of need? Both?
- What are the criteria for placing children on a group, or a personal plan, or both, and who is involved in writing these?
- How are group plans and personal plans compatible with each other?
- How is confidentiality achieved?
- How is the intervention recorded? Register?
- How is progress evaluated? Using what criteria? Who evaluates it?
- How are termly reviews mainly organised and conducted: timings, procedures?
- How are learners and parents prepared for their review?
- Following review, which criteria influence whether children need more, same, or less intervention?

For Response 3:

- What are the criteria for moving children to Response 3?
- What separates intervention at this level from the previous one? (Reflects Local Offer)
- Where does this evidence come from?
- What does this evidence comprise? How is it different from Response 2?
- Who collates this evidence?
- How is it recorded?
- How do the records for SEN Support separate children at Responses 2 and 3?
- Who is responsible for these records?
- Who has a copy? Confidentiality?
- How is progress at this level evaluated? Criteria? Who is involved?
- How are learners and parents prepared for the termly review at this level?
- How are external specialists involved? Reports? Attendance?
- How are these reviews organised and conducted: timing, procedures?
- Following the reviews, which criteria influence whether children need more intensive support, the same for a further term, or less?

At Response 4 (EHCP):

- What are the criteria for moving children to Response 4 (LA assessment)?
- What is the procedure for dealing with requests for LA assessment (parents can request)?
- What is the follow-up procedure where a LA request does not result in an EHCP?
- What is the procedure for a child with a new EHCP?
- Records? Storage? Who has copies?
- How are aspirations/outcomes stated on the EHCP broken down into termly targets?
- How is flexibility and personalisation built into the detailed plan arising from an EHCP?
- What is involved in EHCP-level intervention? How is it more intensive than previously?
- Which children continue to need frequent, regular support from external specialists?
- How do education, health and social services work together, to make the EHCP experience as smooth as possible for children and their families?
- How do children with an EHCP benefit from combined levels of intervention?
- Given that so many specialists may be involved, how is confidentiality maintained?
- How are annual and termly reviews coordinated and how do termly reviews inform annual reviews?
- How is the intervention evaluated? Where does the combined evidence come from for termly and annual reviews?
- What role do external specialists play in reviews? Reports? Attendance?
- How are learners and parents prepared for reviews, particularly annual reviews, and how is it person-centred?
- How are EHCPs kept updated as learners' needs change?
- How are learners' aspirations kept in clear sight throughout their schooling?

For the SENCO:

- What are the criteria for using funding fairly and appropriately, and how is the combined funding (base, notional, other) spread across each response stage?
- How are the benefits evaluated to justify the use of funding?
- How is pupil premium funding used to support pupils who also have SEND?
- How does the whole-school graduated response reflect the school's adapted version of the Local Offer?
- At what point in the graduated response are parents and pupils involved in drafting personal plans?
- From which level of response do the targets start to become more 'additional to and different from' (ATDF) those of children without SEND?
- How does the overall shape of the SEND register (Fig. 2.1), relate to national and similar neighbouring schools? If different, why? (To justify response decisions)
- At each response level, how are learners and parents prepared for transition, and further support beyond school?
- How do the answers to these questions become whole-school policy?
- How are the policy statements reflected in practice *and evaluated*?
- How are these policy statements communicated to parents and other stakeholders?

The Code (DfE/DH 2015, 5.54) lists the main role of the Early Years SENCO as:

- Ensuring practitioners understand their responsibilities towards children with SEND;
- Managing and supporting children with SEND in their setting;
- Advising and supporting colleagues with day-to-day teaching and learning;
- Involving parents;
- Liaising with external specialists where necessary.

The SENCO is also responsible for drafting the Governor's SEN report, to include:

- The types of SEN that the school provides for;
- The school policy on identifying and assessing pupils with SEND;
- How the school consults and involves parents;
- Arrangements for including the child or young person's views;
- Support arrangements for transition (within and beyond the school);
- Approaches to teaching pupils with SEND;
- How a broad and balanced curriculum is made accessible for learners with SEND;
- The expertise and training of all staff who teach pupils with SEND;
- How additional provision is evaluated;
- Inclusion: how pupils with SEND are included in all school activities;
- How the school promotes improvements in social and emotional development;
- How the school prevents/deals with bullying and other types of discrimination;
- How the school includes other agencies, external professionals;
- How the school local offer reflects the LA local offer, and how funding is used fairly.

OFSTED will look closely at how schools specifically promote the achievement of vulnerable groups. The Code states that up to 70% of looked-after children have SEND. Many of these will have an EHCP. The SENCO needs to work closely with designated teachers for looked-after children and other vulnerable pupils.

Chapter summary

This chapter has considered whether a focus on broad areas of need, as opposed to SEN labels, offers a way forward in the quest to improve the statistics listed in Table 1.3.

The chapter has also focused on a fresh approach to the graduated response of the Code, and the need to ensure that good-quality classroom teaching benefits as many children as possible, resulting in fewer learners requiring SEN Support and fewer still, an EHCP, with the kind of targets that are ATDF.

The SENCO role is huge! However, the task is made easier by ensuring that intervention represents the principle of 'fewer and fewer' at each graduated stage. The overall shape should resemble a triangle, as illustrated in Figure 2.1.

The new Code aims to make schools more effective at enabling all children with SEND to succeed. Every school is somewhere along the journey that began with integration failure, but is now rapidly evolving into inclusion success!

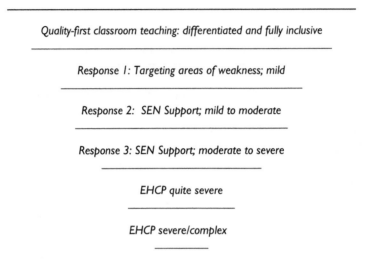

Quality-first classroom teaching: differentiated and fully inclusive

Response 1: Targeting areas of weakness; mild

Response 2: SEN Support; mild to moderate

Response 3: SEN Support; moderate to severe

EHCP quite severe

EHCP severe/complex

Figure 2.1 Ideal shape of SEN intervention

Chapter 3

Special educational needs and disability (SEND)

The relationship between SEN and disability can be problematic, mainly because the distinction between 'disabled' and 'non-disabled' is unclear. This chapter considers:

- The implications of the Equality Act 2010 on schools;
- Who may have a disability;
- Links between SEN and disability;
- The overlap of SEN intervention with 'reasonable adjustments';
- Whole-school responses to disability.

Why disabled people need action

Evidence from the Cabinet Office (2005) suggested that about 7% of the school population is disabled. This percentage includes non-physical disabilities, linked to special educational needs. The report also revealed that:

- 21% of disabled people aged 16–24 had no school qualifications, compared with only 9% of non-disabled in this age range;
- 15% of disabled 16 year olds were out of work, education or training, compared with only 7% of non-disabled peers.

More up-to-date statistics suggest that the situation may have improved slightly (DfE 2014h). For example, the participation of young people in education and training post-KS4 in 2012/13 differed from 85.8% with learning difficulties and disabilities to 90.5% for those without. By age 19, fewer than one-third of pupils with SEND had achieved five GCSEs, compared with about three-quarters of those without: a huge achievement gap. The same report suggested that pupils with SEN and disabilities are still less likely to progress into higher education than other pupils. Absence rates were also particularly high for children and young people with SEND. Interestingly, pupils with sensory difficulties are doing better than those with other types of learning difficulty.

Linking this with the statistics from Table 1.3, underachievement amongst disabled groups is still evident, indicating the need for further urgent action if the life chances of disabled people are to be improved. Life chances begin at school!

The Equality Act

The Equality Act replaces previous legislation (DfE 2014b), but in practice there are few differences in what schools need to do. The Act contains advice for school leaders, staff, governors and SENCOs, whose responsibility it is to provide for the needs of disabled pupils who also have SEN.

The Act sets out legal obligations for schools in terms of admissions, educational provision and exclusions. Schools:

- must not, directly or indirectly, discriminate against disabled pupils;
- must make reasonable adjustments to include disabled pupils in school activities;
- should take *anticipatory* action to prevent disadvantage;
- must promote equality of opportunity;
- must make reasonable adjustments to procedures and practices;
- must publish arrangements for increased access for disabled pupils, in terms of curriculum, physical environment and information.

To comply with the Act, schools' duties are twofold:

- General: to promote equality as part of everyday school activities;
- Specific: to publish accessibility plans that explain how the general duties are achieved.

Table 3.1 illustrates how general duties spill over into school life.

The advice identifies three main differences between former disability legislation and the Equality Act (DfE 2014b):

- The Act does not list day-to-day activities that qualify for disability, and so is less restrictive;
- Institutions cannot justify any failure to put in place reasonable adjustments;
- From September 2012, Local Authorities and schools have been required to provide auxiliary aids and services as reasonable adjustments, where these are not provided by statements (now EHCPs).

The Act carries an assumption that auxiliary aids must be provided by one of the services (education, health, social care) involved in a child's EHCP. These are 'things or persons' which help disabled learners to achieve; for example, hearing loops, adapted keyboards or special software. Items for everyday living, such as hearing aids, are not classed as auxiliary aids because they are not part of any 'reasonable adjustment' to help pupils achieve.

The key test is 'reasonableness', yet the Act does not set out for schools what is reasonable. The Act offers protection for disabled people against being treated less favourably and encourages institutions to treat disabled people *more* favourably, where appropriate, as 'reasonable adjustments' that place disabled pupils *on an equal footing* with non-disabled pupils. Schools are therefore expected to make reasonable changes to their practices, so that disabled pupils benefit from what is on offer *to the same extent* as others without the disability. This implies that in order to treat all pupils *equally*, some pupils may need to be treated *differently*.

Phrases such as 'equal footing' and 'to the same extent' may help SENCOs to think outside the box, to find opportunities for all pupils to learn as equally as is reasonably possible. This does not mean that all

Table 3.1 Schools' general duties under the Equality Act 2010

Schools' general duties	Aspects of school life
Promote equality of opportunity	Access to lessons
Eliminate unlawful discrimination	Bullying in school or in the playground
Eliminate harassment of disabled people	School trips
Promote positive attitudes to disability	Administration of medicines (advice available; DfE 2014f)
Encourage participation by disabled pupils	Exclusions
Take steps to meet the needs of disabled pupils, even if this requires more favourable treatment	Admissions
	Lunchtime supervision and lunch clubs
	Before- or after-school activities and clubs

learners must be enabled to achieve the same outcomes within the same timescales. Children with severe cognitive learning difficulties cannot learn as quickly or as efficiently as their peers. Therefore, *equal treatment through reasonable adjustment* means enabling all learners to achieve their personal best. This is how OFSTED and other stakeholders will view schools' efforts. So, it is important to know what each child's personal best is: to judge success against reasonable adjustments made.

The Act distinguishes between *direct* and *indirect* discrimination. Direct discrimination refers to general duties not to discriminate. Schools can easily overlook discrimination that is indirect — for example, changing a practice that applies to all — which ends up having an inadvertent, adverse effect on the disabled. Schools must guard against doing anything that places disabled pupils at a disadvantage.

Aiming High for Disabled Children highlighted a major transformation (DCSF/DH 2008), based on the vision that families with disabled children should have support to live as ordinarily as possible, with three priorities:

- Access and empowerment: enabling disabled learners and families to be as independent as possible;
- Responsive services, offering timely support;
- Improving quality and capacity.

The Equality Act aims to move all institutions towards this vision.

How is disability defined?

The Act describes disability as a physical or mental impairment which has a long-term and substantial adverse effect on a person's ability to carry out normal day-to-day activities. Key phrases:

- Long term: a year or more
- Substantial: more than minor or trivial
- Adverse effect on normal day-to-day activities.

Disability not only includes obvious physical impairments, but also sensory impairments and many learning difficulties linked to SEN. While physical/sensory disabilities are often straightforward to assess, there is no distinct cut-off point for mental impairment. The distinction — disabled or non-disabled — is one of degree. The Act also specifies many health conditions, such as asthma, cancer, diabetes or epilepsy, as likely disabilities.

Some parents and learners may feel uncomfortable with a disability label, while others see disability as a way of getting their needs met under Equality Act protection. Schools must never identify a child as disabled without agreement from parents. The Special Educational Needs and Disability regulations offer more detailed information for schools (DfE 2014k).

Links between disability and SEN

There is significant overlap between pupils who may be covered by the Equality Act and those who have a SEN, as defined in the Code. Disability does not depend on official diagnosis in the way that a SEN often does. What is 'substantial', or how much of an 'adverse effect' a condition has, is not defined. Not all children who have a SEN are disabled, and not all disabled children have a SEN. Some learners have both. Table 3.2 lists possible examples of overlap.

If SEN is a question of degree, so too is disability, which brings us back to mild, moderate or severe. A child may have a heart condition and be on medication for life, but learning is not affected. A child may break their leg, rendering them temporarily disabled, but again, learning is not affected. A pupil may be unable to write by hand and uses a computer for writing, but other learning is unaffected.

Table 3.2 Examples of overlap between SEN and disability

SEN only	SEN and disability	Disability only
Mild dyslexia	Significant dyspraxia	Asthma
Mild learning difficulties	Severe dyslexia	Physical difficulty
Mild behaviour difficulties	Severe Asperger's	Short stature
Language delay	Severe learning difficulties	Diabetes
	Visual impairment	
	ADHD	

The questions are whether:

- A disability affects learning, requiring special educational provision under the Code;
- A learning difficulty results in the three criteria — substantial; adverse effect on daily life; and long term — thus requiring reasonable adjustments under the Equality Act.

Table 3.3 further exemplifies possible overlap between disability and SEN in terms of the Code. Each individual is different so no rules govern schools' graduated responses.

Table 3.3 Disability and the Code's graduated response

SEN Code response	Disability?	Examples of difficulties
Response 1: targeting weaknesses in class	Highly unlikely	Slight reading delay Not acting on instructions
Response 2: SEN Support without external specialist	Still unlikely, but could develop	Mild learning or behaviour difficulties
Response 3: SEN Support with external specialist	Far more likely	ADHD SEMH Hearing impairment Moderate dyspraxia SLCN
Response 4: EHCP	Almost certainly	Severe learning difficulties Profound and multiple learning difficulties Severe autism

The links between SEN Code responses and disability, as degrees of mild, moderate or severe, are tentative. If in doubt, while never labelling a child 'disabled' without parental agreement, schools would do well to make reasonable adjustments anyway, as part of their inclusion arrangements. Table 3.4 offers case studies to help SENCOs think their way through the links between Code responses and reasonable adjustments.

Questions for SENCOs:

- How is SEN and disability recorded?
- How are learning expectations and aspirations influenced by a perceived disability?
- How does the relationship between SEN and disability guide additional intervention?

Table 3.4 Case studies linking SEN with disability

Michael, Year 9, has an EHCP for SLD. He has limited vocabulary and struggles to communicate verbally. Learning is severely delayed. Michael has medical problems that affect his school day. He is disabled because his SEN difficulties are substantial, long-term and have an adverse effect on daily living.

Jeremy, Year 4, has a significant degree of autism. He struggles with language and communication, and cannot work in a group. SEN provision is at Response 3, involving an external specialist. He has no health problems, and no social-care issues, but his SEN difficulties meet the three criteria for disability.

Seema, Year 2, receives SEN provision at Response 2. She is mildly delayed in most areas of learning, but is expected to catch up. There are no health or social issues. She is not regarded as disabled.

Elise, Year 10, is a wheelchair user, having fallen from a tree at the age of 11. She has achieved above-average expectations, prior to, and since her accident and wishes to study law. She has no learning difficulties that require a Code response. She only needs reasonable adjustments to ensure full access to the curriculum.

Nathan, Year 4, has an EHCP. He has ADHD, moderate learning difficulties and physical difficulties. He can walk with a limp, but cannot run or play physical games. He requires special dentistry, and attends the hospital for leg operations. Nathan receives provision at Response 4, and is regarded as disabled.

Isobel, Year 6, has mild vocabulary and language difficulties. She received speech and language therapy earlier in her schooling, but has now been discharged. She receives Code provision at Response 2, having made good progress throughout her primary school years. Isobel is now only slightly delayed, and is not regarded as disabled.

Making reasonable adjustments

Reasonable adjustments are not that different from SEN responses. The purpose of both is to place pupils on an *equal footing*, or as near as possible, with peers who need neither. Depending on circumstances, the strategies and types of provision in Table 3.5 may represent Code responses, reasonable adjustments, or both. Schools can be reassured that they are highly likely to be covering both legislative areas: the Code and the Equality Act.

Table 3.5 SEN response or reasonable adjustment?

ACCESS. Removing barriers to learning opportunities:
* Simplifying instructions and explanations
* More time for pupils to complete work
* Moving child to front of class
* Pre-teaching tricky words to enable child to access reading book
* A personal mat for a child who struggles to sit still and listen on the carpet
* Visual timetable for pupil with autism
* Social stories for pupils with autism
* Showing pupils with poor memories how to take notes ('jot') effectively
* Scaffolds and models for writing

DIVERSITY. Accommodating different learning styles:
* Allowing pupils with writing difficulties to demonstrate learning by other means
* Visual or kinaesthetic teaching approaches for pupils who find auditory learning hard
* Being flexible with discipline policies for pupils who struggle to conform

CHALLENGE. Making learning objectives and activities appropriate for each learner:
* Backtracking through literacy or numeracy frameworks
* Making challenges deliberately and temporarily easy to encourage independence

SUPPORT ARRANGEMENTS:
* Homework written out by TA for pupil who cannot copy from board
* Computer for child with significant writing difficulties
* Individual workstation for pupil with autism
* Group or individual work with a TA

Behaviour difficulties come under the Equality Act if they relate to an underlying impairment and might be regarded as a SEN/disability if severe. Consider the following:

- A child's parents have split up, causing disruptive behaviour in school;
- A pupil tears up their book and throws it across the classroom;
- A young person hits a teacher or peer;
- A child refuses to write.

The child who refuses to write could have dyslexia and intense frustration. The child whose parents have split up may be only affected temporarily. Each child's circumstance affects the decision: SEN, disability, or both.

Exclusions for children with SEN and/or disabilities are problematic. Only in exceptional circumstances should any pupil with an EHCP be excluded. Schools should also avoid excluding a child with a SEN/disability without an EHCP. Schools should seek advice from a behaviour specialist long before behaviour escalates to the point of possible exclusion. Where exclusion is imminent, a school might ask:

- Is the pupil covered by the Equality Act?
- Is the exclusion related to the pupil's disability? If yes, try to avoid it.
- Would a pupil who is not disabled be excluded for the same behaviour?
- Has everything possible been done, through SEN Support or reasonable adjustments, to address the behaviour?
- Does the exclusion show less favourable treatment?

If reasonable adjustments have been made, and explicit training given to the pupil in how to conform, yet the behaviour has continued, exclusion may be justified. Difficulties arise in cases of severe ADHD, autism and other behavioural disorders. The document 'Mental Health and Behaviour in Schools' (DfE 2015a) offers support.

Accessibility plans: whole-school response

The Equality Act requires schools to examine the impact of all policies on pupils with disabilities; for example, PE, bullying and harassment, SEN, behaviour, after-school clubs, safeguarding.

The accessibility plan should involve all staff, learners with SEN and disabilities, their parents, as well as disabled people in the community, where appropriate. The plan may include:

- How information is made available to pupils/parents with disabilities: brochures, leaflets, letters, emails;
- How the physical environment is adapted to meet disabled needs, perhaps justifiable reasons why it cannot be, or any future intentions to make it more accessible;
- How disabled learners are given complete access to curricular opportunities.

The process may need to happen in stages: research disability needs (learners, staff and parents); involve different groups in writing the plan; implement, evaluate, report on its impact; and adapt the plan accordingly. The first accessibility plans should have been completed by 2010. So, in the light of the Equality Act, the task is to ensure that relevant groups are involved in its ongoing evaluation and development.

Involved groups might include:

- Learners with physical, sensory and learning difficulties, health or medical needs. The groups need to cover the spectrum of SEN and disability across ages;
- Staff with disabilities;
- Parents with learning or physical difficulties. Parents might review the accessibility of information sent home, the timing of reviews, how well reasonable adjustments work for their child, homework or policies that affect disabled pupils;

- External specialists covering the range of physical and mental impairments;
- Community groups that support a range of disabilities.

How might people be encouraged to take part? Staff, parents and learners may be reluctant at first, but an approach that reassures people that disability does not equate with incapability could be the starting point. Once everyone is reassured that the sole intention is to improve the achievement of pupils with disabilities, by placing them on an equal footing with others, contributors to the accessibility plan will feel less threatened. The plan needs to be handled with sensitivity and transparency, focusing on needs, not labels.

Learners could be approached through the School Council, classroom discussions in diversity and difference, or Personal, Health and Social Education (PHSE) lessons. Involving disabled learners in strategies to increase personal access may also stimulate their independence. Involving *all* pupils in policies that affect the disabled could form part of speaking and listening, reading and writing, thus bringing disability into normal school work. Bringing disability into the open by talking about it helps to shift outdated attitudes, and further promote high expectations of disabled learners.

Staff might be approached through staff meetings, followed by individual meetings where appropriate, or by questionnaires.

Parental involvement may take the form of information collected on admission, an initial meeting for all parents, questionnaires (anonymous or not?), evaluation of parents' evenings and school productions.

How does the accessibility plan impact on learners who are also carers? Sensitive reasonable adjustments might include:

- Understanding lateness owing to caring responsibilities;
- More relaxed homework arrangements for known carers;
- Information in a form that is more accessible.

How should schools deal with the accessibility data that emerges? Schools might:

- Sort information into categories of disability;
- Analyse the key issues;
- Draw conclusions and discuss which of the suggested changes have substance. Not all suggestions stem from a disability-based need;
- Which changes require a fresh look at funding? Do some only need creative thinking?
- Which suggested changes can be achieved immediately, or require time to implement?
- Which can be achieved internally, or do some need external specialist support?

Involving a range of people in the accessibility plan could have other positive spin-offs; for example: pupils without disabilities might be encouraged, through understanding, to show greater sensitivity; bullying could be reduced or eliminated; the whole school could develop as a more caring community. Case studies offer insights into the needs of pupils with disabilities. Table 3.6 offers ideas.

Involving learners with and without disabilities in writing and evaluating the accessibility plan and other policies is a challenging but rewarding experience. Staff may be amazed at how much enthusiasm is generated, and how motivating it is for pupils to take part in *genuine* problem-solving, supporting citizenship. Some may need:

- An adult to coach the pupil group;
- Training in the purpose and intended outcomes;
- Training in how to observe classroom practice;
- Teaching how to report their findings.

Table 3.6 Using pupil case studies to inform accessibility plans

Identifying needs:
• What needs arise from the disability?
• Is the disability also a SEN (SEND)?
• If SEND, at which stage of graduated response is this pupil?
• Has every possible reasonable adjustment been identified?

Provision:
• What part does *targeted* classroom differentiation play in addressing the needs?
• What *additional* interventions/reasonable adjustments are provided, and how do these complement the targeted classroom differentiation?
• What does the EHCP (if applicable) offer as top-up education, health and social care?
• How do all three services (if applicable) work together to support outcomes?
• How compatible and seamless are all three levels of provision?

Progression/achievement:
• What is the attainment potential of this learner?
• Are aspirations/expectations high, and shared with relevant staff, parents and pupils?
• Is progress in line with the attainment potential? Are the outcomes met? If not, why not, and which level of support has not worked effectively?
• What else should this learner have achieved, alongside measured attainment?
• Has this pupil been motivated to achieve?
• What evidence supports the evaluation?

The Equality Act aims towards a society of fairness in which disabled pupils are offered the same life chances as non-disabled. Lamb (DCSF 2009e, 6.42), referring to former disability legislation, states: 'there is more work to be done in raising awareness (of disability) … strengthening … of schools' SEN duties.' Schools have come a long way with disability awareness and provision, but the journey is far from over.

Evaluating the accessibility plan and general equality duties

OFSTED places a limiting judgement on schools' effectiveness in providing equality of opportunity, and how schools deal with bullying and harassment. 'Bullying Involving Children with SEN and Disabilities' contains useful strategies to help schools to eliminate bullying (DCSF 2008a). Further advice on tackling bullying in general is also available (DfE 2014g).

How can schools evaluate equality planning and provision? Table 3.7 offers a checklist.

Table 3.7 Evaluating the accessibility plan

Process:
• How transparent is the plan for staff, parents and learners (where appropriate)?
• When is it due for review?
• Who is in charge of the plan?

Content: Does the plan:
• make clear the school's vision and values?
• demonstrate how a range of disabled people have been involved in drafting it?
• identify disabled groups for whom the plan needs to be put into action, and who is responsible for this action?
• contain equality objectives that reflect identified needs or underachievement; for example, to reduce exclusions of black boys, raise results in English for boys, or narrow the achievement gap for *particular* disability types, where this need has been clearly demonstrated (intentional positive discrimination)?
• describe how the school will assess its impact on disability-related policies and practices: bullying, behaviour, exclusion?
• identify priorities for action in terms of: equality of opportunity, eliminating discrimination, harassment and bullying?
• promote positive attitudes towards disabled people, alongside high aspirations?
• encourage full participation of disabled pupils in the life of the school?
• reflect high-quality principles for inclusion?
• involve relevant external specialists to provide training for staff, in support of the plan?

Evaluation: Are there arrangements to:
* monitor the participation and inclusion of disabled learners in school activities?
* monitor and record the attainments and achievements of disabled learners?
* take immediate action where underachievement is observed?
* act on incidents that do not comply with the vision and ethos of the plan?
* include a range of disabled people in its ongoing development, and does the person in charge of the plan communicate regularly with the disabled people for feedback?

The person that has been involved in writing the accessibility plan needs to be involved in evaluating it. The plan should anticipate future admissions of learners with disabilities. Just because a school does not currently have a child with physical difficulties, for instance, does not mean it never will. Schools need to be ready to meet all needs by taking a strategic and wider view of disability in the community.

While this may appear daunting for SENCOs, disability responsibilities do not sit on one or a few shoulders. Both disability and SEN require a whole-school response to the challenges so the accessibility plan could form part of the school development plan.

Chapter summary

This chapter has outlined schools' duties and responsibilities towards disabled children and adults, and considered the overlap between disability and SEN. For pupils with SEND, it is highly likely that where the school delivers an effective graduated response, with full regard to the SEN Code of Practice, that response also conforms to the Equality Act.

Improved outcomes need not always involve additional funding, and solutions to problems do not always involve additional adults. Learners with SEND will achieve better when both disabilities and SEN are seen as challenges rather than problems. Responding to challenges starts with:

* Being flexible, with applied policies and practices;
* Thinking outside the box to find solutions;
* Removing barriers and striving for success;
* Involving SEND learners in their own problem-solving;
* Teaching all learners to be independent;
* High aspirations that separate disability from incapability;
* An 'I can' approach to learning for all.

Involving different groups of disabled and non-disabled learners and adults in the response to challenges enables all of us to gain more insight into disability. Otherwise we cannot presume to understand, much less find solutions to the difficulties that people with disabilities face.

Some years ago I volunteered to assist a visually impaired young man doing an Open University Psychology degree at Warwick University. I was his 'accessibility' adult. As I guided him around the campus, took lecture notes for him and so on, he informed me of many things; for example, he could not judge the fullness of his cup when pouring coffee from a jug. I had never thought about visual impairment affecting depth. Nor could he judge when he came to a kerb; I had to tell him as we approached it, so that he would not overbalance. During that interesting week I felt privileged to gain at least a small insight into that person's day-to-day disability issues.

Gaining insight into disability is a way forward for schools and society.

Providing for the needs of learners with **SEND**

Chapter 4

Inclusion

Access, challenges and barriers

So far in this book we have considered learners with SEND, in terms of who they are and how best to identify their needs through the Code of Practice (DfE/DH 2015), the Equality Act (DfE 2014b), or both. Part II explores provision, starting with inclusion as the basic concept. How can an effective inclusive environment enable all learners to achieve a personal best?

What is inclusion?

Education has moved a long way from original attempts to place children with SEND in mainstream schools, based on the naive assumption that their mere presence would enable them to succeed. Experience has shown otherwise. So where are schools now on this journey towards the kind of inclusion that benefits all learners in mainstream schools (maintained, academy and free), given the still-lingering attainment gap between SEND and non-SEND?

Inclusion for some is about rights. How far is a pupil's right to be educated in mainstream matched by the equal right to be educated in a school that best meets their needs? Mainstream is not *always* compatible. How far can mainstream schools meet the needs of children with profound and multiple learning difficulties (PMLD)? Will special schools always be needed for learners with the most severe types of SEND? Having observed a child with PMLD in a mainstream school, following parental insistence, I believe that common sense must prevail. Every pupil has the right to be educated in a setting that best meets their needs.

One outcome of inclusion is that almost all children with MLD are now educated in the mainstream. Yet, we must still question why only 11% of MLD learners achieved Level 4 in 2009 (Table 1.3), and what happened to the other 89%? Has moving to mainstream education really enabled those pupils to achieve their best?

SENCOs are at the forefront of this particular achievement dilemma. They lead the journey and take much of the responsibility. Having been a SENCO, I understand well the complexities and responsibilities of the role. With regard to their own school's inclusion, SENCOs might ask the following:

- How far are we along the inclusion journey?
- What implications are there for our own policies and practices?
- What are the whole-school characteristics of inclusion? Does our school match up?
- What does total inclusion look like in classrooms? Do our classrooms reflect this?
- What should inclusion look like for learners and parents, and does our school represent a happy and satisfying picture for them?

Inclusion as a social construct could involve the four 'P's:

- Place (mainstream or special school)
- Policy (from Central Government down to LAs and schools)

- Practice (inclusive teaching and learning)
- Personalisation (all pupils benefitting from their experiences and opportunities).

The following sections develop these ideas.

Inclusion as a sense of place

Table 4.1 lists differences between integration and inclusion, illustrating why *place* alone cannot enable SEND learners to succeed in mainstream.

Table 4.1 Place: from integration to inclusion

Integration	Inclusion
Pupils were expected to fit in with the culture and existing curriculum of mainstream schools	Culture and curriculum adapted to meet all learners' needs
Pupils with SEN and disabilities were the responsibility of specialists	All teachers, of every age group or subject, are teachers of SEND
Withdrawal from classroom participation was a common feature of curriculum delivery	Quality first teaching for all learners is the ultimate aim
Areas of a child's life that impacted negatively on achievement were not regarded as the responsibility of educationalists	Well-being is at the forefront of learning, with education, health and social-care professionals all working together
Parents were neither expected, nor supported, to influence educational outcomes for their children	Parent-partnership is now recognised as the key to achievement for learners with SEND, with parents/carers in the centre, rather than on the sidelines
Pupils were not involved in, or expected to take responsibility for their learning	Pupils are at the centre of learning, influencing the content and style of teaching. Self-responsibility is a major goal for all learners.
Labels and low expectations; major killers of achievement	Enlightenment: high aspirations and expectations for every learner
Less emphasis on individuality: pupils with SEN were often regarded as a homogenous group	Personalisation and individuality are recognised as key factors in the high achievement of SEND learners

During the 1980s my role was to support the changed intake of pupils with SEN into Oldham's Local Education Authority (LEA) schools; one, an ex-grammar school. The staff were overwhelmed by what they regarded as pupils who 'should not be there'. These staff members, alongside many others, had not taught children with SEN before, and did not know where to start to meet the needs of children below grammar-school standard. Therefore, changing culture had to happen first, before changes in policy and curricular practice. This anecdote is a reminder that ethos and culture must come first; that *place* represents a belonging, a welcoming and a recognition that all learners are in it together.

Inclusion as whole-school policy

For inclusion to mean success for all, every member of staff, including non-teaching and lunchtime supervisors, must subscribe. The spirit of inclusion that leads to culture change filters down from management, as policy and practice inform and reflect each other.

Key indicators for whole-school inclusion are:

- A mission statement that expresses unconditional acceptance of all learners whose needs can realistically be met in mainstream;
- Policies that embody the mission statement;

- Local mainstream and special schools working together: outreach support, dual placement or training for mainstream staff;
- Every aspect of the curriculum promotes participation and achievement for all;
- All staff on the same wavelength regarding inclusion and striving to achieve it;
- Diversity and difference embraced as a school's strength;
- Use of combined budgets reflecting inclusion principles.

Inclusion works when all staff spray it around everywhere, like air-freshener.

OFSTED (2009b) identified some key features of twelve 'outstanding' secondary schools, noting that these schools were in challenging circumstances yet still highly inclusive. For *every* student the schools had a high regard for:

- Educational progress: seeking the best outcomes for every learner;
- Personal development: the importance of independence and self-responsibility;
- Well-being: recognising that positive emotions underpin effective learning.

The same report noted other common features that contributed to the success of these outstanding schools, including:

- Proving constantly that disadvantage need not limit achievement;
- Putting students first;
- Strong values and high expectations;
- Fulfilment of individual potential through outstanding teaching, rich opportunities and well-targeted support;
- Carefully implemented strategies for removing barriers;
- A high degree of internal consistency;
- Striving towards further improvement;
- Outstanding and well-distributed leadership.

What is well-distributed leadership? Is this management that filters down and permeates all levels of policy and practice? Does it also mean effective delegation that stretches outwards into classrooms? Do leaders 'walk the job' and use their observations to inform and improve policy? SENCOs, as part of the management team, are in a good position to 'walk their job' on behalf of SEND learners.

Whole-school inclusion challenges staff to identify vulnerable groups, some of whom may have SEND, for particular focus; for example, pupils who:

- Are learning English as a second language;
- Have learning difficulties that require SEN provision;
- Have disabilities that require reasonable adjustments;
- Need help to develop social and emotional skills;
- Are looked after by the Local Authority;
- Are from travelling communities;
- Are disadvantaged;
- Are young carers;
- Are gifted and talented.

The schools rated as *outstanding* also paid much attention to the well-being of students, begging the questions: How can sociological factors be compensated for? And how can schools eliminate disadvantage as a justifiable reason for poor attainment?

More recently, OFSTED (2014) has reported that in thirteen local authorities, learners had a less than 50% chance of attending a good or outstanding secondary school. What might be deduced from this potentially alarming statistic? Is the proportion of good or outstanding secondary schools in these authorities less than 50%? Which of the factors listed above that contribute to outstanding and inclusive schools are missing?

To be outstanding, schools' practice must reflect the highest expectations of staff, and the highest aspirations of all learners, including the most able, disabled, and those with SEN. In addition, schools must be consistent, with all staff fully on board and knowing in which direction the school is going towards its inclusion goal.

'Achievement for All' (AfA 2009) is also based around whole-school inclusion. The original project involved ten local authorities, with pupils in Years 1, 5, 7 and 10, including those with SEND. Supported by Lamb (DCSF 2009e), a major emphasis was placed on conversations with parents/carers that shared achievement aspirations. AfA has since been rolled out nationally and challenges schools at policy level to:

- Build structured aspirational conversations with parents into existing staff roles;
- Make these conversations compatible with other parental discussions at reviews.

AfA invites all schools to consider whole-school inclusion issues (see Table 4.2).

Table 4.2 Achievement for All: whole-school issues

VISION:
- To what extent is there a shared vision of high aspirations/expectations for all pupils?
- How do pupils and parents contribute to this vision?
- Is there a common vision and approach to inclusive teaching/learning amongst all staff?

COMMITMENT:
- How extensive is whole-school commitment towards the challenges?
- How relentlessly is the progress of SEND pupils tracked and monitored?
- How well is the culture of inclusion embedded across the whole school at its roots?

COLLABORATION:
- What is the impact of external professional partnerships on SEND outcomes, and where is the evidence?
- How do parents collaborate in their child's learning and school policy?
- How do SEND pupils actively engage with school policies that affect their learning?

COMMUNICATION:
- How effectively do staff communicate with each other, sharing ideas and expertise?
- What systems of safeguarding are in place for vulnerable children?
- What opportunities are there for aspirational conversations with parents and pupils?
- In what ways are SEND (and other) pupils fully involved in decision-making processes?

SENCOs also play a huge part in helping to place vulnerable groups on an equal footing where curriculum policy and practice is concerned. The job has expanded beyond all previous recognition, and involves a lot of collaboration with other managers of vulnerable groups. In tiny schools the SENCO may not have other management support, but there are fewer vulnerable pupils. The inclusion policy needs to make clear which members of staff work together to reflect it in practice.

Inclusion in practice

'Leading on Inclusion' (DfES 2005a) identified three criteria as touchstones for school debate: *presence, participation* and *achievement*. These three criteria continue to underpin good inclusive practice. Table 4.3 considers how these might be identified in classrooms.

Table 4.3 is adapted from criteria originally intended to measure the small step attainment of children working below the National Curriculum (DfEE 2001; DfE 2014i), but may also help schools to measure

Table 4.3 Recognising presence, participation and achievement

PRESENCE:
Pupils are present during the lesson and may encounter things. They may show some awareness of what is happening, but can respond only in the most basic manner. There is no significant learning from the experience and no change for the pupil as a result of being in the lesson.

PARTICIPATION:
Pupils are not only present in the lesson, but using skills of speaking, listening and working in groups. They engage and may feel involved in what is going on by striving to join in, even if learning is minimal. Some small change has taken place, but with little usable understanding of the ideas and concepts.

GAINING SKILLS AND UNDERSTANDING TOWARDS ACHIEVEMENT:
Pupils understand what the lesson is about and are fully included. They gain skills and knowledge that they can transfer into other areas of learning: in social skills, literacy or numeracy. Achievement from the content of the lesson can be clearly demonstrated. Change has taken place.

inclusion in practice. Pupils may be present in classrooms without any learning outcome, but if no bridge connects such presence with participation and achievement what has been the point? The criteria suggest that, for all pupils, there should be some recognisable and beneficial *change* as a result of being in a lesson. Consider the following scenarios:

1. A Year 8 student with SLD is supported in Maths by a TA who tries to interpret for him what the teacher is explaining to the class about algebraic equations. The TA tries to explain this, with no success. The learning challenge is too high. This pupil does not interact with others, and during group work his group consists of himself and the TA. At the end of this lesson there has been no change in learning.
2. A child with visual impairment needs reading materials in enlarged font but in some lessons this is not provided, so the child cannot participate.
3. A pupil with autism sits outside the classroom. Occasionally, the TA comes out to check that he is copying his spellings correctly, but with no focus on how to actually learn them. There is no participation in classroom work.
4. The objectives for a science lesson are to observe and report on chemical changes. Some SEN pupils observe the changes but cannot report them in writing, so they draw the changes or describe them to a TA. These pupils are present, participating and to some extent, achieving. There is some recognisable change by the end of the lesson.
5. As part of a topic on World War II, pupils work in groups, debating whether or not life in Nazi Germany was better or worse than before Hitler. Despite the valiant efforts of the TA, one pupil does not understand the language, or the concepts surrounding the debate. At the end of the lesson this pupil cannot recall anything about it. No change. No learning. Much frustration!

Schools need to question whether inclusion means that pupils should be in class lessons 100% of the time, even if challenges are unreachable. Can all lessons be made accessible? Perhaps not. If presence, participation and achievement are sound criteria by which to judge effective inclusion, then what needs to happen? If occasionally, lessons may be seen as a waste of time for students with severe SEND, would being withdrawn to participate in something else be a better option? Inclusion does not necessitate 100% presence in class, with no achievement as the end result. Placing pupils in lessons that are completely beyond them not only wastes precious learning time, but reduces learners' capacity to demonstrate what they *can* do. In addition, presence alone encourages learners with SEND to accept lack of understanding as normal, when we should be educating them to recognise their misunderstandings and correct them. Presence alone limits pupil independence and reduces the effectiveness of a pupil's innate abilities because of the huge barriers placed in front of them.

Inclusion at classroom level is a major challenge. Classroom teaching is multi-tasking at its extreme, like juggling many balls in the air at once. The data in Table 1.3, supported by other evidence (DfE 2014h), proves that presence alone cannot deliver, so how can the long tail of underachievement be considerably shortened? Teaching and learning must be further joined up, for *all* children.

Let's start with inclusion at first base: *quality first teaching (QFT)*. 'Learning and Teaching for Children with SEN in Primary School' (DfES 2004b), later applied to social and emotional contexts (DfES 2005b), explored a three-part strategy that applies to every key stage: learning objectives, learning styles and access (see Table 4.4). These interrelated strategies characterise inclusion within the whole class. As they interact, presence, participation and achievement follow. Is this the key to joined-up teaching and learning for all?

Table 4.4 Characteristics of class inclusion

Learning objectives	Setting appropriate challenges for all pupils
Learning styles	Responding to different ways of learning
Access	Overcoming potential barriers to learning

Setting appropriate challenges for learning means backtracking through learning objectives to find simpler levels within the same theme, as with the examples in Table 4.5. Juggling many balls in the air is more difficult when they are different weights and sizes. And so with learning. I cannot imagine trying to teach thirty children different skills along different themes. So, if the whole class is doing addition, it seems simpler to address a single theme at different levels, according to pupils' numerical understanding. Such backtracking enables teachers to set challenges that are neither historic (too easy), nor too idealistic (unreachable), and may also help teachers to maintain their sanity while trying to meet everyone's needs at once.

How might backtracking for objectives work in practice? It may facilitate:

- A more inclusive start, with all pupils listening and attending, before moving off at various points, to begin their work, with a TA helping to start off each group.
- Pupils working on differentiated objectives along the common theme: in groups, independently or with support from a class-based teaching assistant.
- More easily prepared and collated resources.
- All learners joining in with the plenary/conclusion.

Table 4.5 Backtracking along a common learning theme

FRACTIONS:
- Understand halves and quarters
- Find half, quarter and three-quarters of shapes, then of small amounts (half of 8)
- Understand simple fractions (one-third, one-fifth), then multiple (two-thirds, six-tenths)
- Relate parts to wholes, then to mixed and improper fractions
- Match equivalent fractions of the same value
- Match fractions to decimals; order them on a number line
- Add, subtract, multiply and divide fractions … and so on

ADDITION:
- Add numbers up to 5, then to 10, then to 20
- Add numbers to 50, then to 100 with no 'carrying'
- Add numbers to 100 with 'carrying'
- Add numbers to 1,000 … and so on

ENGAGING WITH, AND RESPONDING TO, TEXTS:
- Choose books to read and explain why
- Share and compare choices of reading
- Read favourite authors, and experiment with others to compare writing styles
- Plan personal reading goals … and so on

Most learning themes can be backtracked. Even algebra can be simplified to the idea of missing numbers (24 - ? = 20), as I observed in one lesson for a pupil with SLD. That learner was made to feel included, although he knew that his level of work was different.

It is difficult to simplify lessons where the conceptual ideas are too complex. How, for example, could the history teacher have simplified the debate on Nazi Germany (example 5 above)? Even in the interests of inclusion, maybe teachers can't do it *every* time.

What about the second of our three strategies from Table 4.4: diversity of learning styles? The three main styles of learning are now accepted as auditory, visual and kinaesthetic, to which I add a fourth: social. Although most of us learn through a mixture of all four, some people, especially with SEND, often learn better through one channel than the other three. For example, many pupils with autism do not like working socially. Some pupils with SLCN may struggle with auditory learning.

The visual and kinaesthetic channels tend to be favoured. Learners achieve better through their preferred style, but need to learn through other styles also. Mixing them throughout lessons, with due emphasis on individual preferences, takes teachers a step further towards effective inclusion. Table 4.6 illustrates this with fractions and writing.

Learning styles merit more in-depth classroom exploration. Most lessons feature auditory learning: teachers talk; learners listen. The problem is that some pupils cannot listen for too long before becoming bored and distracted. So through a flexible mix of learning styles teachers can liven up lessons and engage more learners.

The third classroom inclusion strategy is access: removing the barriers that prevent SEND learners from being on an 'equal footing'. What do *barriers* mean for the learners who experience them? A barrier may be social and emotional: Dad in prison; Mum an alcoholic. The physical or sensory barriers are more obvious. Then there are learning barriers that obscure communication between teachers and pupils; for example, SLCN or ASD. And what about the child who cannot concentrate because they are hungry: the barrier of disadvantage?

How can such barriers be removed, or compensated for, by schools? Breakfast clubs and free school meals have long been used to alleviate disadvantage. Moving position in the classroom, or special chairs help with physical barriers. Tools and specialised equipment support sensory barriers. Schools can do little to deal with home circumstances, except create a learning environment that soothes emotions and tries to compensate where it can.

Table 4.6 Addressing learning styles

STORY WRITING:	
Visual	• Drawing out the story first
	• Pictures to stimulate plot/characters
Auditory	• Sharing ideas
	• Oral story starters
	• Sounds to convey mood/atmosphere
Kinaesthetic	• Sequencing word cards
	• Acting out scenes from stories
	• Using the computer to write
Social	• Making up stories in pairs
	• Sharing each other's stories
FRACTIONS:	
Visual	• Colouring fraction parts in shapes
	• Drawing fractions
	• Colouring parts of pictures (half of 6 cats)
Auditory	• Mental work on fraction problems
Kinaesthetic	• Matching fraction pieces to form wholes
	• Using counters or objects to share into fractional parts
	• Cutting shapes into fractions
Social	• Talking about fractions: larger or smaller
	• Why is 'one-third' so called?
	• Playing card games: Snap, Happy Families, dominoes, pairs

Barriers can also be caused by hidden problems: poor working memory, inadequate vocabulary, inability to work with others or being slow to process information. Table 4.7 illustrates some barriers that tend to obscure learning opportunities.

Table 4.7 Removing barriers to learning: examples of strategies

Inadequate vocabulary?	**Slow to process verbal information?**
• Make it a priority in every lesson	• Slow down when speaking
• Explain technical subject vocabulary	• Stress verbs and other meaning words
• Make the thesaurus a word tool	• Summarise instructions and explanations
• Set up talking groups to debate and problem-solve	• Sharpen listening skills
• Pre-teach words in early readers	
Poor working memory?	**Self-esteem blocking confidence?**
• Teach effective jotting and note-taking	• Seize on and use known strengths
• Play games that stimulate memory	• Use praise and rewards sensitively
• Use visual aids to compensate	• Build confidence through a no-fail approach
• Don't overload memory	• Make all tasks reachable
• Allow some pupils to use tables squares to ease their problems	• Stress the 'I can' approach
Slow to complete work?	**Emotions blocking off learning? Try:**
• Allow more time if genuinely needed	• Mentoring at intervals throughout the day
• Use timers to structure working time	• Peer-buddying
• Reduce volume of writing	• Circle time
• Prompt pupils part-way through tasks	• Counselling
• Make task completion a clear objective	• Child and Adolescent Mental Health Service (CAMHS) may be needed
Can't work with others? Teach in small achievable steps:	**Reluctant to write?**
• With one friend	• Reduce size of task
• With a different peer	• Mark or correct errors sensitively
• With a younger or older child	• Find something to praise before pointing out errors
• Change type of task gradually	• Allow choice of tasks when possible
• Increase group size gradually	• Make editing/crossings-out positive
	• Reduce unnecessary copying
	• Draw storyline first
	• Write in pairs
	• Use scaffolds/templates

In practice, adapting objectives, addressing learning styles and removing access barriers all merge together. When does an access barrier become an adapted pupil challenge, or vice versa? How do these strategies interact to enhance learning? Answers to such questions could bring teachers closer to developing their personal style of inclusivity.

Inclusion as personal experience

Chapter 2 briefly explored personalisation as individual quirks of character and personalities. For many pupils personalisation is icing on the cake; a sweetener. Personalisation also helps teachers to know particular learners' needs in more insightful ways than SEN labels or broad areas of need. For pupils who are disadvantaged, including those with SEND, personalisation may mean 'wrap-around care'.

Personalisation may represent the *value* of experiences that pupils take from lessons. For example:

- A feel-good factor.
- A swelling of pride as a child runs from the classroom after a good lesson.
- Has a pupil just solved a problem? Has the learning penny just dropped?
- Has a five-minute chat helped to lift a child's mood and avoid confrontation?
- Has a child received a reward for good work as something they particularly value?

SEND support strategies are often highly personalised; for instance, social stories for pupils with autism. Although social stories have a common structure, each story is personalised to the individual.

Finally, personalisation involves a two-way channel of communication. No longer do teachers teach and pupils learn in one direction only. Learners teach educators about themselves to further inform the teaching strategies that support their learning. This personalisation cycle holds the key to narrowing that elusive achievement gap.

Chapter summary

This chapter has explored four 'P's that facilitate successful inclusion — place, policy, practice and personalisation — and has hopefully presented schools (mainly SENCOs) with starting points for debate. How do presence, participation and achievement fit with learning objectives, styles and access? Are these concepts helpful for teachers still searching for that elusive judgement of *outstanding?* The answers are contextual as no two schools are the same. What works for one may not work in exactly the same way for another. Teachers need to teach to their individual style.

Inclusion is not therefore, a matter of creating a template for staff to follow. If this was the case, then teaching would be unrealistically simplified to a 'painting by numbers' approach, leaving little scope for the inspirational uniqueness that each teacher brings to the collective endeavour.

The ideas presented have hopefully inspired the kind of debate that will take schools closer to their personal inclusion quest. In my view, most schools have come a long way with place and policy, but have further to go with practice and personalisation.

Chapter 5

Inclusion for all

Having explored inclusion per se through place, policy, practice and personalisation, this chapter considers its ideological implications 'for all', and asks:

- How has the the Inclusion Development Plan (IDP) influenced inclusion, and where are schools *now*?
- What is the long-term vision?
- How can Achievement for All move schools further towards seamless inclusion?

The Inclusion Development Plan (IDP)

OFSTED (2006) concluded that the educational setting (special or mainstream) makes little difference to how pupils with SEND achieve. What matters is the quality of teaching and learning in either environment. 'Removing Barriers to Achievement' had stipulated previously that inclusion is 'much more than the type of school that children attend' and the 'quality of their experience', and that children should 'participate fully in the life of the school' (DfES 2004a). The Inclusion Development Programme (IDP) was its response.

The IDP sought to further link inclusive policy with practice (DCSF 2008c). The Bercow Report (2007) highlighted SLCN. This IDP component also recommended other publications, including *Speaking and Listening for All* (Edwards 1999), that still offers a wealth of practical, inclusive strategies for supporting language/communication. The Steer Report (2009) focused on behaviour. Both reports stressed the need for more inclusive approaches.

The IDP emerged also as an outcome of the Lamb Inquiry that expressed a need for all teachers to become better-trained in SEN (DCSF 2009e). The programme first focused on training resources to improve outcomes for children with SLCN (DCSF 2008d), dyslexia, autism (2009b, c) and behavioural, emotional and social difficulties (BESD) (2010a, b) — now SEMH. The entire training programme signified a national initiative to reshape QFT by focusing on these common SEN types. Table 5.1 lists areas of teacher self-evaluation adapted from the original staff audit.

The IDP was intended to involve staff at every level — teaching assistants, class and subject teachers, managers and heads — recognising that 'walking the job' only works when managers know what to look for.

The currently updated programme aims to ensure that teaching:

- Is set within a culture of high expectations and aspirations;
- Focuses on what children learn, rather than activities they do;
- Is based on prior assessment of what learners know, understand and can do;
- Uses teaching approaches that engage all children.

Although the initial IDP materials featured four areas of SEN, the emphasis was on improved teaching and learning *for all*. So why these four? Two of these areas had already been brought to attention by reports (Bercow 2007; Steer 2009), and represent a high incidence of SEN in many classrooms and are also

Table 5.1 Stages of pre-knowledge for staff audit, adapted from National Strategies Inclusion Development Programme

Skills and knowledge	Focusing	Developing	Establishing	Enhancing	Evidence
I identify needs	X	X	X	X	
I know my learners	X	X	X	X	
I use advice		X	X	X	
I recognise barriers		X	X	X	
I adapt lesson plans		X	X	X	
I use pupil voice			X	X	
I monitor all progress			X	X	
I collaborate to improve practice			X	X	
All my pupils make good progress				X	

interlinked. Children with autism, for example, are likely to have behaviour difficulties, often arising from an aspect of SLCN. The focus on dyslexia also supports other children with literacy difficulties. The original IDP choices recognised SEN coexistence: the aim being perhaps to gain maximum goals from a few well-aimed shots into the inclusion net.

Now fast forward: the IDP has been developed and extended to take schools further towards inclusion *for all*. The refreshed materials are available at www.idponline.org.uk. New resources have been added at Master's level, including autism, MLD, BESD (now SEMH), SpLD and SLCN. These are areas of SEN that Lamb (DCSF 2009e) thought teachers should know most about (see www.advanced-training.org.uk).

A third set of IDP resources emerged through the Salt Review (2010) that highlighted a lack of well-trained teachers in complex areas of SEN, mainly SLD and PMLD, and was supported by work from the Complex Learning Difficulties and Disabilities Research Project 2009–11 (Carpenter et al. 2011). These materials comprise sixteen modules, available at www.complexneeds.org.uk. All of these resources continue to support the narrowing of the achievement gap, reinforcing the notion of success 'for all'.

Schools, guided by SENCOs, now need to evaluate where they are in relation to the areas listed in Table 5.1. Self-evaluation questions might now include:

- How far have teachers progressed along the IDP judgement levels?
- How accurate are teachers' self-evaluations compared with manager observations?
- Has there been a measurable difference in progress amongst IDP learner groups?
- Are other outcomes evident: motivation, independence, discipline, attitudes to work?
- What has the IDP achieved so far for the whole school?

The IDP has proved itself a valuable training tool, but this can only continue if teachers are given time and resources to experiment in full collaboration with colleagues.

It is interesting that the staff audit (Table 5.1) places lesson *planning* at the early stage of *developing* skills and knowledge, prior to using pupil voice at the *establishing* stage. How far has 'pupil voice' become established in classrooms, as a result of the IDP?

Table 5.2 offers a means of planning, based on knowing what learners can or cannot do, according to the *specific content* of lessons. The model rests on the following principles:

- Learners' personal outcomes are influenced by the lesson's conceptual demands;
- Some learners with cognitive difficulties (for example, SLD) may progress sideways, with more practice at the core stage, as others progress into the development stage;
- High, open-ended expectations are balanced against knowing all learners' capabilities;
- Teacher and class TA manage learning together;
- All learners are trained to work independently for varying periods of time;
- Discipline is well established.

Table 5.2 Planning: core, development and enrichment

Lesson stages of delivery	Adult interaction
CORE: All learners introduced to core ideas, and engaged in first set of tasks	1 Teacher introduces lesson for all 2 Teacher/TA manage core activities
DEVELOPMENT: Majority of learners engaged in tasks or activities	3 Teacher begins developmental stage while TA manages pupils at core stage 4 Teacher and TA manage core and development, assessing/monitoring
ENRICHMENT: A few learners engaged in enrichment discussion or activities	5 Teacher introduces enriched activities while TA manages core/development 6 Teacher and TA manage all three stages together
SUMMARY:	Both adults summarise lesson and point out positive achievements

Without these underlying principles, such a model cannot work. Of course, it is too simplistic in its present form: pupils may need pre-core material, with more backtracking. Similarly, not all learners at the development level will do the same activities. Even enrichment activities may slightly differ. Each of the three levels may need to mushroom out, from pre-core to multi-development to super-enrichment. The model offers a starting point: the bare bones of planning *for all,* ready for those crucial personalisation touches.

The Complex Learning Difficulties and Disabilities (CLDD) research focused on learners' engagement as the main success factor in any lesson (Carpenter *et al.* 2011). A problem has always been how to avoid some children listening too much, becoming restless, before switching off completely. The model in Table 5.2 may relieve children from the tedium of listening (often without understanding) to overlong introductions, as the least able listen only to what they need (core) before starting their simplified tasks. The model also helps to solve the problem of able children not being stretched enough (enrichment).

Table 5.3 outlines two secondary examples, based on the stages in Table 5.2.

Table 5.3 Building learning from a core base

Context and lesson	Core base for all	Development for majority	Enrichment for a few
Comparing England with Malawi: Year 8 Geography	Pupils look at photo of Malawi. Class discussion of same and different. Pupils talk in pairs about what they see, then write it up. A few children need tools to support writing (key words). Initial introduction for all shows clear differences between both countries.	Comparison extended to include data on areas: Malawi/England; larger/smaller? While 'core' learners are still using the picture, these pupils talk in pairs about what further differences they can identify from other sources.	The comparison is further extended for the few who finish more quickly; data on geographical areas is compared with population to compare population density.
Algebra: Year 8 Maths	All pupils introduced to the idea of missing numbers; class discussion of how to work them out. A few children need counters to visualise problem, and use smaller number range.	Majority move on to using letters for numbers: x and y. Some core children may not be ready for abstract approach yet.	More advanced algebraic equations for those who are ready to expand the ideas.

Most lessons that can be stranded — from simple, to more difficult, to complex — fit the model in Table 5.2. For example:

- Addition: core group to 20; development to 100; enrichment beyond;
- Fractions: core, halves/quarters; development, simple fractions; enrichment, multiple fractions;
- Sentence work: core, simple; development, connectives; enrichment, clauses;
- Phonics: core – consonant, vowel, consonant (CVC); development – consonant, consonant, vowel, consonant/consonant, vowel, consonant, consonant (CCVC/CVCC); enrichment – vowel digraphs.

How can teachers adapt lessons that contain difficult conceptual content, such as that on Nazi Germany mentioned earlier? Such lessons involve complex, abstract concepts built on the necessary understanding of simpler ones. If the underlying concepts are not secure, the barriers for learners are huge, perhaps insurmountable. In such circumstances, teachers have not failed to include all learners — the challenges may simply be too high for a minority — and no learner can afford to waste precious learning time.

At the opposite end of the planning spectrum, pupils achieve simply by outcome, working at their own level; for example:

- Working in pairs to describe things, by colour, size and shape;
- Writing stories on a topic of their own choice;
- Sorting pictures into categories;
- Open-ended numeracy: 'Tell me about number 25'. Responses may range amongst 20 + 5, 100 - 75, 12.5 × 2 or 10% of 250.

Achievement by outcome offers adults the chance to observe/assess where individual learners have reached.

The IDP has been in action for some years, focusing on QFT, yet evidence suggests that inclusion is still not quite where it needs to be. The IDP drew attention to the fact that classroom teaching is a highly skilled, multi-task job, managing people (highly challenging), as well as systems. Yet, how well does society regard teachers as *managers* of learning, in charge of potentially high productivity, with high-stake economic and social outcomes for future society? How far is total quality inclusion feasible with current teacher/TA/learner ratios, given the increasing diversity of classroom populations, with a higher incidence of CLDD children in mainstream classrooms (Carpenter *et al.* 2011)? Such thorny questions need to be posed.

Alongside the IDP, programmes include the SEND Pathfinder Champion (DfE 2014j). Information packs, are available to download and contain helpful resources, SEN case studies and feedback from the implementation of SEND reforms. Supported by the Council for Disabled Children, this programme now operates across nine regions (as regional leads), focusing on all schools 'Delivering Better Outcomes Together'.

The IDP has set the inclusion ball rolling! How fast can schools keep up with it?

A vision for all

The 2020 vision is one in which 'all children and young people achieve higher standards and gaps in average attainment between different groups … are reduced … [The] system must focus more strongly on the progress of all …' (DfES 2006b). The report further expresses the need for 'high-quality, challenging teaching that engages pupils and helps them to take ownership' (DfES 2006b, p. 41). As I write, we are five years from the vision and much has happened during the last nine. Learners with SEND have made slow, steady improvement, but schools are again at the forefront of huge change. How can this vision be realised?

The vision refers to *challenge, engagement* and *ownership*. Should this be where educationalists now focus their attention, posing questions for schools that focus on 'for all' rather than SEND only? Would teachers now benefit from using the skills and knowledge about SEND, gained from IDP improved practice, to branch out towards seamless inclusion *for all*? If so:

- How do schools challenge all learners together?
- How can teachers engage them all?
- How can *all* learners be encouraged to take ownership?

This shift in emphasis, onto learners, can only happen if schools state these goals as part of their overall vision and move forward as whole organisations towards reshaping classroom teaching.

Barriers and benefits of 'for all'

Identifying needs and *knowing learners* represented 'focusing' on the IDP staff audit (Table 5.1). Learning needs affect classroom dynamics, through cause and consequence. Placing a pupil with a behaviour difficulty with the wrong peers, or failing to ensure all members of a group have the capacity to 'gel', can wreck a most brilliantly planned lesson.

How might learners perceive the 'for all' challenge? For example, if some pupils are allowed to write less, could this affect the motivation, hence engagement, of those who are made to write more? If some children are allowed extra time for tasks, could this cause resentment amongst others? All learners need to be helped to understand the 'for all' concept. Furthermore, equality of opportunity often means some pupils with SEND being taught differently. How might this affect overall engagement? Have all children been helped to understand why some receive extra in the form of tools or time with adults?

Referring back to SEN types, and the broad areas of need (communication/interaction, cognition/learning, social/behavioural, sensory/physical), how well do these suit the expanded notion of 'for all'? Problems with working memory, for example, affect many types of SEN, so memory work benefits others without SEN who also struggle to keep up.

What about the vision towards pupil ownership? Assuming all learners have become challenged and engaged, how can they be helped to take on self-ownership of progress? Joseph, Year 10, has a statement (soon to be EHCP), and is on track for either a C or B in English and Maths GCSE. I regularly ask him what he has done or learned. His responses are often 'don't know' or 'can't remember', or a shrug of the shoulders. Joseph has still not grasped that, at Year 10, he is mainly in charge! I encourage him to tell me about misunderstandings so that I can reflect our tutor sessions from his school experiences. He rarely does. I have managed to get Joseph to think about *why* we are doing something and to tell me when he does not understand. Alongside many learners, with and without SEND, he has been conditioned to 'receive' learning rather than actively *search* for it (*to* rather than *with*). The roots of self-ownership should have been planted in primary school.

Self-ownership and independence are crucial to closing the achievement gap. The 'for all' concept depends on all learners working as independently as possible, so that teachers can step back and do what the Code requests of them as learning managers: Assess, Plan, Do and Review. Chapter 12 focuses on pupil voice (IDP audit level: establishing and enhancing) and independence. At this point, I am reminded of a quote from the poet, William Yeats: 'Education is not filling a bucket, but lighting a fire!'

Achievement for All (AfA): Impact?

What lessons does AfA have for 2015 onwards, towards the 2020 vision? The Achievement for All two-year pilot is now national (AfA 2009). Its three aims are aspiration, access and achievement. AfA has also been extended to Post 16.

A University of Manchester seminar (Humphrey and Squires, 2012) summarised the success of AfA through:

- Assessment, tracking and intervention;
- Structured conversations with parents, one per term;
- Provision for wider outcomes: attendance, bullying, positive relationships and participation in school life.

Conversations with parents have been crucial to the success of AfA, arising from Lamb's view that parents and children are central (DCSF 2009e).

Evidence from the AfA evaluation (Humphrey and Squires 2013) has been both quantitative (teacher/parent surveys and attendance data) and qualitative (interviews and pupil case studies). The AfA report for 2013/14 concluded that over a short time AfA has made a powerful impact on school improvement in the following ways (AfA 2014):

- AfA pupils in each pilot year (1, 5, 7 and 10) made better progress in English and Maths than others with SEND nationally;
- Pupils in Years 1, 5 and 10 also made more progress in English and Maths than pupils *without* SEND nationally;
- Schools reporting excellent relationships with parents had risen from 12% to 48%;
- Attendance increased, personal relationships improved, and bullying decreased.

Blanchford (2015) further describes AfA as 'common-sensing' the Code and refers to the Child and Families Bill (DfE 2014a) as, 'enabling all schools to benefit from the highly successful AfA approach', and that it 'reflects key features ... in the Code of Practice'. AfA may represent a 'quiet revolution', but requires, as Blanchford put it, 'deep-diving' into learner data to search out implications for teaching. SENCOs are also reminded that the pupil premium can be used to fund AfA.

Finally, the Learners First: School Partnership (www.learnersfirst.net) was formed in 2012 as a supportive network of school leaders, linked to AfA. The partnership aims towards building excellence and addressing underperformance so that:

- All pupils make at least 'good' progress;
- There are no underperforming cohorts;
- All teachers deliver at least 'good' teaching;
- All schools are moving to at least the next level of successful performance.

The Partnership operates with 'teaching schools' assigned to train and support others, with a sharp focus on leadership linked with QFT. Teaching schools must:

- Have an *outstanding* rating from OFSTED;
- Show excellent leadership;
- Be prepared to work with others to provide high-quality training and development.

By 2016 the Government aims to have 600 'teaching schools' within the network. Maybe yours is an AfA school or part of the network. If not, could it benefit from this kind of mutually supportive approach?

Chapter summary

This chapter has expanded on the general concept of inclusion by outlining strategies to develop classroom practice through whole-school leadership — the IDP and AfA — and speculated on the 2020 educational vision.

Why have the IDP and AfA featured together here? Because classroom practice must reflect whole-school policy. Success in reshaping QFT depends on *whole-school thrusts* of managerial energy radiating throughout all educational settings.

For *all* learners to make 'at least good progress' teachers need more than training. They need time, open minds and confidence to be involved in their own QFT research. All classrooms need wide-open doors for fresh ideas to blow in!

Where are SENCOs in the collective chain of inclusive effort? Do they have a foot in both camps, policy and practice, in a way that some leaders whose focus is not entirely on SEND, do not? Key questions in our schools are:

- Does policy influence practice? Is the direction of change mainly 'top down'?
- Does practice feed policy? Is change directed mainly from 'bottom up'?
- Does the direction of change stem from a healthy atmosphere of trust, flowing in both directions?

The answers to these questions influence how SENCOs 'walk their job'. If teachers are to engage in the 'for all' movement they need support and encouragement, beyond judgement.

The aim of 'at least good progress for all learners' relies on 'at least good teaching' from all teachers, who, like learners, need rewards for their efforts!

Finally, from the old vision of integration (special into mainstream) a new vision of achievement 'for all' has emerged. From an initial focus on 'placement', with numerous examples of failure, the new vision represents success. Integration began as a worthy aim, but based on a naive (at that time) assumption of the task that schools faced.

How many children *cannot* progress? Zero! Such aspirational thinking summarises inclusion 'for all'.

Chapter 6

Intervention
Towards a complete package

The previous two chapters focused on QFT and the whole-school thrust towards achievement for all. Is it reasonable to assume that teachers, as a result of IDP training, now judge their practice as *establishing*, or even *enhancing*, with *evidence* to demonstrate it (Table 5.1)? Is classroom inclusion now mainly embedded and prepared for the additional intervention that makes QFT part of a complete learning package?

The IDP focus should have established for all learners:

- A sense of belonging
- Teaching/learning and peer relationships
- Classroom routines and social disciplines
- Strategies for independent working.

QFT is the foundation for well-being, participation and achievement. Without it, whatever else a learner experiences at school has minimal impact. The more effective QFT is, the less need for additional intervention. So for pupils with mild learning difficulties, *more* effective QFT may result in *less* SEN.

Even the best QFT cannot enable *all* children to reach their potential. The diversity of inclusion implies that:

- Pupils learn at varying rates, regardless of teachers' pedagogical excellence;
- Some pupils, especially with cognitive difficulties, always need to revisit learning experiences to reinforce them.

It is useful to reflect that QFT is so called because it is the first crucial step, though not the complete package. Some children will always need additional intervention.

Waves of intervention

The three-wave model offers a solid framework for combining QFT with the Code's graduated response (DfE 2011a). Given that QFT is the responsibility of class teachers, and that any intervention 'additional to and different from' is more the responsibility of SENCOs, it is worth reflecting on how they combine into a complete package.

Table 6.1 illustrates the Waves Model, which invites schools to ask how this fits with the ideas and concepts considered earlier (SEN types, four areas of need, graduated responses and degrees of intervention). How does the Waves Model enable teachers and SENCOs to intervene collaboratively? Crucially, at what point does QFT cross over into additional intervention? This last question is important because crossover partly determines:

- Whose responsibility: class teacher or SENCO.
- The use of funding: core, notional SEN or EHCP top up.
- The deployment of additional adults.
- Quality assurance and evaluation of all staff.

Table 6.1 The three-wave model

Wave 1	Wave 2	Wave 3
Quality first teaching (QFT) for every learner	QFT plus interventions for some pupils that enable them to keep up with age-related expectations	QFT plus interventions that are more personalised and intensive for the few, including those with an EHCP

Table 6.2 offers examples of how 'waves' intervention relates to SEN, but only by knowing *learners* (perhaps from AfA 'deep diving') can the right decisions be made. How can these ideas combine to make the effects of AfA a reality, relying as it does, on a smooth continuum of intervention? What schools do not want is a situation where staff absolve responsibility for any part of the complete package. Waves are not separate: they flow into, affect and support each other through the turbulence — as should all members of staff.

Table 6.2 Linking Waves provision with SEN

SEN Type	Areas of need	Wave 1: QFT Code Response 1	Wave 2: QFT + Code Responses 2 to 3	Wave 3: QFT + Code Responses 3 to 4 (EHCP)
SLD SLCN	Cognition, severe Communication and interaction	Objectives backtracked Simplified tasks Visual aids Applied speech and language therapy (SALT)	Group work: phonics, vocabulary and social skills	1–1 writing/maths Speech and language therapy (SALT)
MLD	Cognition, moderate	Objectives backtracked Simplified tasks Visual aids	Group work: Phonics Comprehension Independence	Advice from external specialist may apply
SLCN	Communication and interaction	Adapted language Communication	Group work: Vocabulary Sentence work	Speech and language therapy may be needed
ASD	Cognition, mild Communication and interaction	Some backtracking Seating change	Group work: Social skills	Depends on whether mild, moderate or severe
Dyslexia	Cognition, specific	Some backtracking Multisensory approaches	Work on phonics and writing skills	May not apply, depends on degree
SEMH	Communication and interaction	Adapted routine Behaviour plan, sanction/reward	Work on emotional barriers	Depends on degree of difficulty
ADHD	Communication and interaction	Applied for concentration		
Dyspraxia	Cognition, specific	Computer for writing	Handwriting work	Depends on severity
Hearing or Visual	Sensory	Removal of access barriers: seating, materials?	Depends on severity	Depends on severity
Physical	Physical	Removal of access barriers: seating, timing	Depends on severity	Depends on severity

Table 6.2 illustrates some of the challenges that SENCOs and class teachers face together, for example:

- Pupils with multiple, coexisting types of SEND.
- How do the waves relate to SEND, as mild, moderate or severe?
- What particular features differentiate each wave as a support strategy: group or individual? External specialist advice?
- How are waves 2/3 interventions reinforced/practised as part of QFT? For example, a Speech and Language Therapy (SALT) programme, or a social skills programme?
- How do EHCPs permeate through the Waves Model, from intervention at Code Response 4 to QFT level?
- How are wave interventions balanced to reflect needs? More or less of 1, 2 or 3?

The essential difference between what happens as QFT — adaptation, reinforcement or compensation within the classroom — and additional interventions that develop skills and knowledge out of the classroom, influences the use of funding. It is for SENCOs to mainly decide how the notional SEN budget is to be fairly spent, and to justify their decisions to parents, leader colleagues and governors.

The criteria for placing individuals at a specific wave level and justifying this in relation to the Code Response and the Equality Act, need to be stated as policy. At the same time, criteria are rarely black or white and SEND learners often represent grey areas. According to which level of policy-stated criteria, do more intensive interventions under 'SEN Support' slide from Code Response 2 to 3, and so require external specialist advice? The EHCP is easier, being an LA decision, yet how is intervention at Wave 3 clearly differentiated between children with and without an EHCP? Clear, yet flexible, criteria for linking the Code's graduated response with reasonable adjustments and the Waves Model of delivery need to be part of SEND policy.

Should the next stage of training, for *teachers and SENCOs together,* aim to make the Waves Model as effective as possible? The IDP and AfA have provided the starting point. The Waves Model has huge potential to turn the right key further in the lock.

Why is smoothly blended wave provision more likely to result in maximum achievement? Reasons:

- What is taught must be practised: additional group or individual work out of the classroom is of little use without reinforcement in its natural learning context;
- Educationalists recognise that excellent QFT alone cannot produce the best achievement for all;
- Most learning is hierarchical, built brick by brick, from a range of learning experiences;
- Learners need to see their learning as a whole package, not as disjointed bits.

The whole package relies on excellent communication amongst teachers, other adults and SENCOs. Parents also need to be a central part of the Waves package and to know which bits of their child's intervention fit where.

Pupils also need to see learning as the big picture, not jigsaw pieces. A child who works with a TA on reading comprehension needs to practise these skills back in class. Similarly, learners need to feel confident that additional work on spelling/writing will be reinforced by their class teacher.

QFT or intervention?

So how do SENCOs and class teachers decide which provision is part of QFT and what is 'additional to and different from' (ATDF)? Examples:

- An IT reading intervention programme;
- Five minutes daily with a TA to practise spellings;
- Early literacy support for Year 1 children delayed with phonics;

- 30 minutes with TA three times per week on numeracy;
- 30 minutes with TA daily on GCSE study strategies;
- Paired reading or writing for a pupil in Year 2 with a pupil in Year 6;
- 10 minutes each day with a Year head for behaviour issues.

All of the above support learning, but are they QFT or SEN Support? SENCOs might ask:

- How ATDF is the support strategy?
- Does it require additional staffing? If so, does it support all children or certain ones?
- How expensive is it?
- Does the support strategy focus on skills that few children need (social, self-help), or on classroom routines for all?
- Does the support strategy focus on academic learning or other skills, music or art therapy, perhaps to boost a learner's self-esteem?
- Does it support access to normal lessons?
- Does the strategy support children on a temporary basis, who are expected to catch up, as opposed to learners who will always need intervention?

SENCOs will come up with different answers, but this is such a grey area that it doesn't matter so long as the school can fully justify its decisions.

Waves 2 and 3 structured interventions

Some Wave 2 structured interventions aimed to secure learning for children who had fallen behind in primary school, and included the 'Every Child' programmes:

- Every Child a Reader (ECaR; DfES 2006c), targeted at Year 1 low achievers;
- Every Child a Writer (ECaW; DCSF 2009h), targeted at Year 3/4 children;
- Every Child a Talker (ECaT; DCSF 2008e), targeted at early years;
- Every Child Counts (ECC; DfE 2011b), targeted at Year 2 low achievers.

These programmes formed a key part of the National Strategies that aimed for all children to be on track with literacy and maths by the end of Key Stage 2.

Since national roll-out, many Local Authorities now operate these programmes in some form, providing literacy and numeracy training for teachers and TAs. Some schools (for example, Shadsworth Infant School, Blackburn) have become ECaR literacy centres. ECaW trainers (for example, Emma Rogers; see Useful websites) offer training in classrooms on modelling, problem-solving and feedback, to improve whole-class work on writing, as well as guided writing for groups.

An evaluation of Worcestershire's ECaT programme 2009–2013, concluded that confidence and knowledge amongst early years practitioners had increased from 44% to 95%, with practitioners better able to identify potential SLCN (Worcestershire Health and NHS Trust 2013). These gains are likely to be more widely reflected. As a result of the ECaT programme, early years settings and schools now recognise the crucial importance of language/communication at every stage.

A report on the teaching of early reading (Rose 2006) stated that intervention should:

- Not replace systematic teaching of phonics and related reading strategies at Wave 1;
- Be based on accurate assessment of phonic development;
- Be early enough to prevent embedded literacy failure;
- Have clear entry and exit criteria.

Wave 2 approaches have worked largely because interventions have been implemented early enough to prevent failure. However, evaluation of the Every Child Counts programme points out the comparatively high cost in relation to the moderate gains made (DfE 2011b). Other Wave 2 structured interventions have included the Springboard programmes and 'Overcoming Barriers' for different year groups (TES 2011). Whilst some schools may still have these materials, their overall usefulness is now limited, owing to the new National Curriculum and the abandonment of the old assessment levels. However, they continue to support the hierarchical development of literacy and numeracy.

An evaluation of National Strategy interventions suggested that interventions have been more successful at primary level than secondary (OFSTED 2009a). No single intervention had been successful in every school studied. The report concluded that quality of management was a far more determining factor in intervention success: a key message for SENCOs.

A further problem with Wave 2 structured interventions is that they rely on programmes being followed precisely, and not necessarily on the teaching skills of the TAs who deliver them. The lack of clear links between the intervention programme and class lessons has often resulted in disjointed learning. The evaluation report also alluded to TAs' lack of subject knowledge, and limited flexibility in meeting pupils' needs through Wave 2 interventions (OFSTED 2009a).

Wave 3 interventions have mainly involved more flexible strategies for children:

- Who need individual support;
- Who progress in very small steps;
- Who receive Wave 2 intervention in literacy/numeracy but need individual intervention in areas such as communication or behavioural skills.

Structured programmes to support Wave 3 have included:
- Reading Recovery (see Useful websites): the individual version of ECaR;
- Catch-up literacy (see Useful websites at end of book).

A study of Reading Recovery (RR) in London schools concluded that RR had been 'highly successful' and that the lowest achieving children in Year 1 had made four times the normal rate of progress throughout the year (Burroughs-Lange and Douetil 2006, p. 3). Furthermore, those children who had accessed RR had been enabled, through their increased gains (averaging 20 months, compared with 7 months), to access Year 2 reading at text level far more effectively than their non-RR peers. The benefits of RR are also highly likely to be reflected widely.

Of course, most packages work well when one-to-one, so are such gains merely the result of additional staffing, or the structured nature of the programmes? Probably both. Reading intervention needs a trained literacy teacher (or TA) to ensure best results. As a literacy specialist, I believe that catching up with reading and writing cannot simply involve 'practice makes perfect'. The skills involved are complex and often caused by barriers that need to be broken through before progress can be made.

Whether an intervention is Wave 2 or Wave 3 is less important than ensuring that a particular intervention works for individual children. Evaluations of literacy intervention (Brooks 2007, 2013) suggest that:

- Ordinary teaching alone does not enable children with literacy difficulties to catch up;
- Schemes for literacy must be highly structured (reflecting hierarchical pathways);
- Comprehension skills can be improved when directly targeted;
- ICT approaches work best when directly targeted;
- Interventions should aim to double the average rate of progress.

Given that both studies by Brooks (2007, 2013) arrived at similar conclusions, what can schools take from this research? The reports suggest teachers often overestimate dyslexia and that many children have early literacy difficulties that are not dyslexic. Brooks suggests two tests that could raise the accuracy of teachers' judgements. These are:

- Sound isolation: measuring phonemic awareness; plus
- Either rapid naming of colours (verbal processing speed) or letter knowledge.

These tests, Brooks suggests, if done early in Year 1, could be more helpful than the phonic screening tests introduced in England in 2012, which, the report states, 42% of children initially failed! The difference between early reading difficulties and dyslexia remains vitally important for SENCOs and class teachers managing the Waves Model.

Brooks (2013) also drew attention to the sparsity of intervention schemes for KS3, but mentioned 'Grammar for Writing' as having potential. The report recognised that the literacy demands of secondary schools rapidly increase beyond those of primary. Do secondary SENCOs, together with English teachers, need to focus more on children catching up with language and literacy skills, as preparation for secondary English?

Research on what works for children with mathematical difficulties concluded that no two learners with mathematical difficulties are the same, emphasising individual approaches (Dowker 2009). As with literacy, ordinary maths teaching alone will not allow children with significant numeracy difficulties to catch up. Dowker concluded that interventions which focus on 'components with which individual children have difficulties' are more effective than those that assume all difficulties are similar. Therefore, interventions at Waves 2 and 3 must be precisely targeted.

My conclusions are that structured programmes for Waves 2 and 3 benefit most learners but not all. It is easy for schools to place a child on a programme already structured for countless 'unknowns', for a TA to simply follow. It is worth ensuring that some of the TA workforce is trained sufficiently in literacy and numeracy to:

- Design and run intervention based on *known* learners' needs;
- Break down literacy or numeracy barriers that have caused delay;
- Reflect intervention back to QFT.

The individuality of intervention is of crucial importance to children who are significantly delayed. Whether designed as 'catch up' or 'close up' (of the achievement gap), successful intervention depends on knowing learners' needs.

Getting intervention together

Interventions are only effective when synchronised with personal plans. The *timing* of a structured intervention for language, literacy or numeracy, with entry and exit criteria, is important. For evaluation, it needs to roughly match the review dates for personal plan (IEP) and EHCP reviews.

An important difference between personal plans and interventions is that the former only features priority areas of need, whereas the latter should include any *area* of learning difficulty that limits achievement, spread *across all three waves*. Personal plans therefore only record a small part of the total intervention package.

Interventions are intended to reduce high numbers of children being inappropriately assessed as SEN. Some struggling learners only need intervention long enough to catch up. One term could unblock a problem. Consider, for example:

- A bereaved child who needs temporary emotional support;
- A child with a broken leg, who is temporarily disabled;
- A child whose confidence needs to be boosted to put them back on track.

These types of problems need intervention as part of the Waves Model, but do not necessarily match the criteria for SEN or disability.

On the other hand, some learners will always need something additional to the normal curriculum. Many children, once placed onto the old-style SEN register, remained on it throughout schooling, floating aimlessly between outdated categories of School Action/School Action Plus. Has such long-term intervention been ineffective, or have these children really had some long-standing form of SEN? Will a few children *always* need extra, whatever QFT they receive? Yes, but the problem lies in identifying which children:

- Only need one or two terms of intervention, to catch up and keep up;
- Need intervention that depends on the topic being taught: flexible;
- Need ongoing intervention to maintain average achievement;
- Will always need intervention to achieve their best, even when *best* is likely to remain below average.

Only for children with the most severe difficulties should intervention ever become a lifestyle. Ideally, it should also be needs-led rather than resource-led. Not all interventions need additional financing. The dilemma for SENCOs and teachers together lies in not only deciding between QFT and SEN, but also when intervention is no longer needed, and QFT alone can take over.

SENCOs also need to recognise where, within the flow of wave interventions, reasonable adjustments feature, as they need to be evaluated under the Equality Act. Examples of disability intervention that may not require funding include:

- Allowing a secondary wheelchair-user to leave lessons early to avoid crowd problems;
- Providing enlarged font for a visually impaired pupil;
- Allowing a parent to support an anxious child with a hearing impairment in the classroom for a few minutes each day;
- Allowing a student to work at a separate workstation;
- Adapted seating arrangements.

Should a particular intervention be changed regularly to rekindle interest? I think so. Motivation is a prime factor.

As SENCOs are also aware, evaluations apply to almost everything schools do. So how should interventions be evaluated? Table 6.3 offers a checklist.

The questions in Table 6.3 reflect the need for schools to get as much value for money out of each as possible. A key outcome is whether or not the skills and knowledge gained are used frequently and reinforced in other learning contexts. How successful has an intervention been if:

- A child does well on a structured spelling programme, but does not reflect the gains through independent writing?
- A pupil has successfully learned maths facts, including times tables, but does not use them in maths lessons?
- A learner has worked on social skills but does not transfer them to class group work?

The only true test of long-term value is for learners to transfer Wave 2 and 3 structured interventions into their wider contexts.

A further dilemma is whether withdrawing a child from class for additional intervention benefits learning more than joining in with the class lesson. Intervention is always a balancing act of gains and losses. Taking a child out from something they love may cause resentment. Given that inclusion is measured by the criteria of presence, participation and achievement, it can be argued that by removing the opportunity for a child to participate in a class lesson, inclusion is therefore compromised. On the other hand, if a child is gaining nothing from the lesson, is intervention therefore supporting inclusion? Common sense must prevail!

Table 6.3 Setting up and evaluating interventions

SETTING UP:
- What is the intervention intended to achieve (the goal)? Expected rate of progress?
- Does it match the needs of the child?
- Where does it sit within the flow of the Waves Model, reinforced through QFT?
- Is the overall gain from the intervention programme likely to be worth more than what the child is missing from the class lesson?
- Where does the intervention sit in relation to the Code graduated response, or as a reasonable adjustment for disability?
- Does the child's personal plan form part of this intervention? If so, how are the personal plan (PP) targets and strategies matched to those of the intervention?
- Is there an assigned adult in charge of the intervention?
- Do all relevant staff know about it (including subject teachers)?
- Have both parents and child been informed and helped to support it?
- What are the arrangements for monitoring progress? Evidence?
- What is the timescale?

EVALUATING:
- Have goals been achieved and expected progress made?
- If not, can the reason be justified; for example, extensive pupil absence?
- Is the evidence consistent, and from different areas of the curriculum?
- Is the pupil using the skills/knowledge gained in other subjects across the curriculum?
- How likely is it that the gain can be maintained? Should the intervention be ceased? Changed? Continued? If ceased, how is longer-term sustainability to be measured?

Chapter summary

The seamless interaction of Waves 1, 2 and 3 may appear more complex than it actually is. Once staff get their heads around the ideas and come to understand their duties under the Code and the Equality Act, blending each idea into a combined three-part flow happens naturally.

The three waves represent how the Code and the Equality Act are applied in schools. Can getting the waves together narrow that achievement gap? I believe it can, but only when staff are willing to share errors, as well as successes, in the interests of creative research. The Waves Model may also need a sprinkling of personalisation for some learners, to add that magic touch.

Chapter 7

Learning through personalisation

Students, young people, pupils, learners, children! I have used these nouns to refer collectively to humans that attend schools and educational settings. But who are they? Society has a natural tendency to lump individuals together: workers, employees, management, public sector, lower/middle class. Similarly, education sorts young humans into key stages, year groups, categories, sets, types, as well as SEND, in order for schools and settings to organise what they do. Within this necessary organisation, where and how does personalisation fit?

This chapter asks:

- What is personalisation and how can schools find it?
- Why do some learners need it?
- Which pupils need a more personalised approach?
- How can school personalisation work?
- How could personalisation support achievement for all?
- How might meeting personalisation needs slot into the SENCO role?

What is personalisation and why do schools need it?

To what extent do you agree with the following? Personalisation:

- Is the opposite of stereotyping
- Supports high aspirations
- May shorten that long tail of underachievement
- Recognises unique characteristics of individuals
- Recognises that pupils with SEND are not a homogenous group of learners
- Aims to find differences within commonalities
- Motivates and encourages all learners to give their best.

Through the IDP and AfA, most schools now know more about SEND learners and how to include their needs alongside peers. Huge improvements have already been made.

So, as a result of the input, should the output now be all children achieving? Yes, but statistics still suggest otherwise, proving that education cannot boil down to input and output. So what else is needed? Could personalisation add that magic touch to make the difference between failure and success? If so, why? Personalisation:

- Reaches parts (of learners) that other teaching strategies do not reach;
- Touches the beating heart of the person inside a 'type'.

Personalisation also recognises that learners are *not*:

- Numbers on statistical charts
- Entries on SEN Support lists
- Members of a 'SEND table' of children in a classroom
- Parts of a group receiving the same intervention programme.

Schools have already tried teaching SEND learners by commonality (SEN type or Code areas of need) with partial success. Is it time to further recognise differences for those who are harder to teach than the rest of the school population? And should schools investigate what makes particular children 'hard to teach', without clustering their uniqueness into a further commonality?

Outcomes from personalised approaches could include:

- Improved well-being: more children enjoying school and feeling relaxed;
- Improved motivation, independence and self-responsibility;
- Reduced absence;
- Reduced incidents of challenging behaviour, and exclusions;
- Young people better equipped for work and adult life;
- Further narrowing of the achievement gap.

Schools would reap huge benefits from pupil motivation. Instead of teaching dragging learning behind it, could learning somehow lead teaching through improved pupil motivation and involvement? Such an aim is within reach. Personalisation could make a vital difference to overall results.

How does personalisation differ from QFT differentiation? Godfrey's (2015) view that differentiation moves from lesson to child, whereas personalisation moves from child to lesson, summarises this subtle difference.

What type of learning environment supports personalisation? Is it:

- Valuing ALL progress, however far removed from age-related thresholds?
- Ceasing to compare learners against each other?
- Making all children feel safe and cared for?
- Promoting confidence through the 'I can' approach?
- Promoting full engagement and participation in the *life* of the school or setting?
- Celebrating broader achievements? Music? Art? Sport?
- Eliminating self-perceptions of failure?
- Recognising the richness that diversity offers?
- Compensating for vulnerability: SEND, looked after, disadvantaged, English as an Additional Language (EAL)?
- Making pupils and parents *equal partners*?

It is all of these. What parents know about their children and what learners know about themselves represents a huge fountain of information to tap into. The above factors invite schools to place at least equal value on areas of well-being, from which curricular achievement naturally follows.

Finding personalisation

Traditionally, schools have focused on English and Mathematics as measures of success. 'Pedagogy and Personalisation' suggested that every learner should succeed from a standpoint of high expectations (DfES 2007). Have those who did not achieve age-related levels therefore failed? Did those learners self-believe their failure?

Where are the pressure points for individuals? 'Progression Guidance' (DCSF 2009f) stated that all learners should make at least two levels of progress (under the old curriculum) through a key stage, and that pupils with SEND, working below average, should also achieve this rate. Was this rate of progress realistic for *all* of the pupils who lagged behind? If it was, then why have so many SEND learners fallen short? Where it has been unrealistic, could such pressure have increased some learners' anxiety to succeed? Can insensitive pressure encourage a child to switch off? I think it can. Now that the old levels have been abandoned, it remains to be seen what rate of progress will be expected for learners with SEND, as all pupils follow the new curriculum.

To what extent is personalisation achieved through pedagogical excellence? Does pedagogy underpin QFT for all, and the success of the three-wave model? If so, how? 'Pedagogy and Personalisation' identified four related domains that help teachers to consider teaching approaches (DfES 2007). These are listed in Table 7.1. Where, within these domains, does personalisation hide?

Personalisation is present within all domains, but is it equally spread? Maybe knowledge of the subject sometimes leads. Perhaps, for certain lessons, the teaching model is most important. Maybe the skills of working with learners dominate if a child with behaviour problems plays up. Furthermore, do conditions for learning underpin the other three at all times? Yes, because learners' feelings and emotions govern outcomes, from positives — pride, interest, satisfaction or excitement — to negatives: anger, frustration, apathy or boredom. Emotions rule in all classrooms.

With regard to pedagogy, improved outcomes for teachers would include:

- Raising attainment for pupils at the tail end;
- Having access to the best resources and ideas at their fingertips;
- Better understanding of progression in language, literacy and mathematics;
- Time to follow through the assess–plan–do–review cycle thoroughly.

Rarely is there enough time for teachers to evaluate the impact of pedagogical approaches on individual learners. Is this a job for SENCOs: to observe targeted learners in class and feed back, sharing ideas in order to build pedagogical excellence, as well as develop collaborative colleague relationships?

Table 7.2 considers pedagogical approaches from both perspectives: teaching and learning. Problems from learners' perspectives may also include other factors, such as:

- I'm hungry; had no breakfast;
- Can't be bothered to work it out;
- Mum and Dad had a big row last night. What if they split up?
- I hate maths! It's boring!

Table 7.1 Interrelated domains of pedagogy

Curriculum and subject knowledge: • Key concepts/language that define subject topics • Progress within subjects • Which models of teaching and learning best match the subject • How literacy, maths and ICT skills support the subject	Teaching repertoire of skills and techniques that demand active engagement: • Competency in planning and structuring learning • Skills of questioning, guiding, coaching and organising group work • Skills of working with learners
Teaching and learning models: • Direct teaching: for acquiring new skills and knowledge • Hierarchical sequences: literacy/maths • Cognitive models: to process information, build concepts, using enquiry, analysis, investigation • Social models: for learner collaboration and problem-solving	Conditions for learning: • Managing class, groups, pairs • Building inclusive interaction with learners • Ensuring that learning builds onto prior learning and attainment • Effective use of time, space and resources for the benefit of all learners

Table 7.2 Teaching from learners' perspectives

Year 6 sentence work: Construct sentences in different ways to express subtle distinctions of meaning	Year 6: division and problem-solving: • What is 52 divided by 6? • How many bricks (each 20cm long) are needed to build a wall 3m in length and 4 layers of bricks high?
Problems for teachers: • Choosing the teaching models that suit this objective • Understanding the sentence skills that precede it • Engaging learners with sentence writing • Planning for learners who can achieve it • Backtracking for those who are not yet ready for this level	Problems for teachers: • Choosing the most suitable teaching model • Understanding the preceding multiplication skills • Getting all children to understand the key concept of the lesson (multiplication) • Backtracking the numeracy levels for those who need it
Problems for learners: • Where do my sentences begin and end? • I can only write short sentences • I can write some complex sentences but I need a scaffold • I don't understand the objective • What do I have to do? • Which words make my meanings different?	Problems for learners: • What does divide mean? • What does the sign mean? • How do I divide? • I don't know my times tables. • What do cm and m mean? • How many cm in a metre? • What does 'remainder' mean? What do I do with it? Decimal or fraction? • I don't understand the problem. • Which sum(s) do I choose? Why? • How many steps to the problem? • Which step do I work out first? • I've forgotten where I'm up to.

Does looking at lessons from the perspective of different learners help to head off problems before they arise? If learners were asked to give feedback on some lessons would the range of comments illuminate conflicting issues and strengthen teaching/learning relationships? I believe they would. Besides, in this age of feedback and evaluation for everything else in life, why should feedback not apply to the 'consumers' of teaching?

How might mainstream teachers use these pedagogical domains to develop personalisation for individuals who are 'hard to teach'? Are there strands of training within each domain, to support the personalisation quest that go beyond inclusion? Perhaps this is where teachers in special schools could support those in mainstream.

What is meant by 'hard to teach'? Most teachers will quickly name children who fall under this description. Would they include learners who:

- Do not listen to instructions, causing adults to repeat them?
- Forget what they have to do, perhaps requiring tasks written down?
- Work so slowly that tasks are rarely finished, making it difficult to assess learning?
- Cannot concentrate for long, causing disruption if not dealt with?
- Struggle to grasp new concepts easily, needing teaching from a range of angles?
- Struggle to remember skills and information from one lesson to the next, needing continual overlap and reinforcement?

Teaching will always include children who are easier or harder to teach than others. Is the trick to always have a Plan B? Are we back to knowing the learners? Yet, how can all teachers, particularly secondary subject teachers, know all of the personal ins and outs of the children they teach?

This is where parents come in. Do they represent Plan B? Do parents hold the key to knowing why some learners are harder to teach, and why, for their child, teaching does not easily result in learning? AfA relies on structured conversations with parents. Should parent/teacher conversations for the 'harder to teach' extend beyond regular parental discussions, in an attempt to find out where teaching and learning can hook up?

Finally, how do learners' emotions feature? Do some learners need to *feel* learning? Could the 'feel good' factor move personalisation forward? Does it include:

- Never being allowed to experience failure?
- Knowing and celebrating progress?
- Being engaged, interested and productive in lessons *most* of the time?
- Sharing in each other's success?
- Sharing success with parents, and reaping rewards from home?

Personalisation is not easy to find, but is worth searching for.

Taking a broader look at personal achievement

So far, we have considered personalisation in terms of finding an elusive *something* that enables hard-to-teach individuals to achieve in ways that measure success: *attainment*.

Would celebrating broader achievement also support attainment? Some examples:

- A 'school-phobic' pupil on home tuition manages school for five lessons per week;
- A learner with ASD manages a group-based task;
- A child who refuses to write excels in the school football team (writes about football?);
- A young carer completes homework in difficult circumstances;
- A child manages to work without a TA for 20 minutes;
- A truant from a disadvantaged background improves attendance;
- A Year 7 child with SLD finds their own way around secondary school;
- A child finds the courage to report bullying.

Considering personalisation from broader perspectives, as huge problems that learners overcome, may enable schools to meet them part-way, recognising achievement on their terms as a starting point, coaxing them towards the kind of achievement that schools desire.

Some achievements have little to do with school per se. On a school trip to an outward-bound centre in the Lakes, a pupil who had been an utter behavioural pain, showed a side of himself that I had never seen before: watching over younger kids in the party, and generally falling over himself to tidy up and be helpful. Following that week-long trip, I harnessed that 'need to be helpful' in class, and eventually turned it into a more harmonious and productive teacher/learner relationship.

A second example: a Year 5 child with ADHD and cognitive difficulties (with EHCP) plays the keyboard in a 'band'. The little group of friends meet at his home and practise in the cellar. Imagine the din! Yet, this different side of a 'hard to teach' child has been harnessed: he now plays the piano to welcome parents into school parent evenings and events.

Chapter summary

Personalisation within the pedagogy of teaching adds a further ingredient to the achievement mix. Figure 7.1 illustrates how personalised strategies slice through other considerations, reflecting the 'for all' principle, and permeating levels of identification and provision. Could schools, especially larger ones, cope with such flexibility and possible distance between policy and practice? Is personalisation practical only for a few learners with SEND? Only schools know how personalisation might work for them.

Is personalisation becoming closer to pupil voice as schools strive to meet some learners on their own terms? Making allowances need not contradict basic disciplines and routines. Nor does personalisation

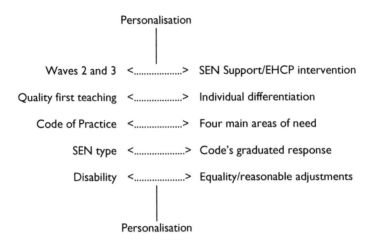

Figure 7.1 Personalisation: part of the achievement mix

equate with reduced expectations. At its heart lies the principle that all learners need to be themselves, provided that others are not adversely affected. Personalisation often results in learners better able to make changes in learning habits and/or behaviour that schools ultimately seek, so both sides benefit.

I have used the term 'hard to teach', not simply in a behavioural sense, as many children who fail to achieve are models of classroom compliance. 'Hard to teach' refers to pupils for whom teaching fails to find a way through to learning, so could personalisation help to narrow the achievement gap?

Achievement *in* school often means learners overcoming problems *out of* school: their *well-being*. Personalisation celebrates 'off-the-wall', alternative achievement, as well as that which is conventional and measurable.

'Breaking the Link' stated that when personalised learning is part of a whole-school approach, 'planning and teaching match the needs of all pupils, reducing the need to define children according to categories of need' (DCSF 2010c, p. 2). Thus, personalisation may prevent some children needing SEN Support.

Personalisation involves psychology: getting children onto 'our' side; schools going the extra mile to seek out hidden potential, such as an alternative strength, a particular learning style, a strong emotion. AfA necessitates a huge shake-out of the relationship between teaching and learning. Personalisation has the potential to make every young person's learning experience stretching, creative, fun and successful.

Part of the responsibility lies with SENCOs through their support of QFT and wave interventions. SENCOs who can step back from day-to-day SEND engagement (and constant pressure) to think *creatively* about what is possible, however odd, stand a greater chance of influencing personalisation, and narrowing that stubborn achievement gap.

Chapter 8

Provision-mapping

This chapter looks at:

- What provision maps do and why schools need them;
- How provision-mapping simplifies SEND management into a single process;
- How provision maps match funding streams;
- How personal plans relate to provision-mapping;
- Different models.

What is a provision map and why do schools need one?

Provision-mapping was introduced through 'Leading on Inclusion' (DfES 2005a) to manage ATDF provision, and was followed by 'Your Child, Your School, Our Future' (DCSF 2009d) that promoted it as a means of ending low achievement for learners with SEND. Since 2012 there has been a legal requirement to publish information on how a school's pupil premium has been spent (DfE 2012). Provision maps enable schools to do all of these.

A provision map offers schools a common direction towards an agreed destination, helping to keep track of:

- What is provided over and above QFT
- Which learners receive additional provision
- How budgets are spent
- Who delivers what; justifying staff deployment
- How schools comply with relevant legislation.

Provision-mapping represents the big picture towards which everyone subscribes: staff, external specialists, parents, learners. A provision map enables schools to match teaching resources with costs to learning outcomes.

The Code states that provision maps should show *all* provision over and above the normal curriculum (ATDF). It is therefore essential for SENCOs to know the difference.

The Code also reminds us that OFSTED needs to see:

- Evidence of progress;
- A focus on outcomes;
- A rigorous monitoring and evaluation of any SEN support provided.

Provision maps have the potential to do all of the above, and also:

- Inform annual and termly reviews by incorporating personal plans;
- Summarise the collation of evidence for learners who need EHCP assessment;

- Lead to school improvement;
- Support schools in improving their core offer;
- Enable schools to check and update additional provision easily;
- Support pupil and parental conversations.

So if provision maps can do everything, it is worth investing to make them super- effective and efficient.

Developing a provision map: The process

Who is involved in developing the provision map? 'Leading on Inclusion' suggested all staff who manage additional funding: head, senior leaders, SENCO, coordinators of vulnerable groups/pastoral support (DfES 2005a). Provision-mapping is a whole-school task.

Provision-mapping ensures all additional funding is used fairly and transparently to deliver personalised outcomes. This requires coordinators of funding streams to work strategically to direct resources where needed. All staff are involved in collecting data that indicates how funding should be appropriately spread.

The provision map, for individuals, must take account of parents' and pupils' views on:

- The type of provision and how it is delivered. One-to-one; structured intervention; group?
- The roles they play in ensuring success.

Where are its parameters? Does the provision map cover:

- SEN provision alone?
- Reasonable adjustments?
- Other funding for vulnerable groups?
- Personalised approaches 'outside the box'?

Can a provision map include everything on one document without defeating its purpose (to simplify procedures)? If not, what other documentation supplements it: QFT records, notes on personalised approaches, personal plans?

Needs-led or resource-led? Ideally provision should be needs-led, with the capacity to meet more needs, be more personalised and promote parental confidence. On the other hand, finances may not stretch as far as needs demand. If resource-led, provision is more likely to stay within the budget, but less likely to reflect changing needs over time, and far less likely to satisfy all parents. The task is to find middle ground that represents fairness.

Provision maps must be:

- Easily manageable for the teams responsible for their effectiveness;
- As personalised as is practicable;
- Transparent for staff;
- Confidential for parental discussions;
- The basis of monitoring/evaluation, for individual pupils and collective school results.

Provision-mapping might start with an audit of learning needs across the school. Examples of primary needs are:

- High numbers of children entering Reception with poor language and/or social skills;
- Significant numeracy difficulties in Year 1;
- A group in Year 2 with poor phonic skills;
- A group in Year 3 whose attainment has dipped following transition;

- A problem with behaviour in Year 5;
- Poor reading comprehension in Year 6.

In secondary, problems might be:

- A low attainment group in Year 7, causing concern amongst subject teachers;
- Year 9 learners with significant learning difficulties that are being bullied;
- Pockets of EAL across year groups, needing intensive work on speaking and listening;
- Other needs: for example, absence in Year 9; or pupils who need a breakfast club.

What else might be revealed? Auditing may highlight other learning issues: social and communication; memory difficulties; or pockets of low self-esteem. How do schools prioritise spending for such diverse needs? Auditing may also indicate school-based needs, such as staff development, resource problems or a need to change whole-school strategy. Auditing is an opportunity for a whole school to learn about itself.

Auditing annually encourages schools to break away from familiar and outdated approaches to problem-solving. Repetitive use of the same strategies/resources smother the creative and visionary thinking that good provision-mapping requires.

Following an audit, the provision map is likely to include learners:

- Receiving provision through SEN Support;
- Receiving SEN Support with EHCP top up;
- With disabilities, needing reasonable adjustments (perhaps auxiliary aids);
- In vulnerable groups, receiving support from the pupil premium or other funding;
- With other needs that require personalised approaches.

This diverse range of *individual* learning needs may highlight key stage or year group *patterns,* such as the primary and secondary examples listed above. Patterns of need help to structure the provision map, with staff training to support it. Given these two audit outcomes (patterning, plus individual needs *within* those patterns), how does a school design a provision map, based on its unique circumstances and population of learners? Table 8.1 offers a process.

The provision map represents all staff travelling in the *same* direction, with an *agreed* agenda. The collective journey has a:

- Starting point: all learners who are not making progress through QFT alone;
- Route: economical range of time-limited interventions and support strategies;
- Destination: expected outcomes and criteria for success.

Provision maps lend structure and organisational togetherness to the Code's requirement to assess, plan, do, review. Ideally the provision map should be evaluated and updated annually, in the light of each year's pupil achievement data.

The provision map also helps to inform annual reports for parents and supports the Code of Practice suggestion that some schools may wish to report more frequently, for example, termly, for some pupils with significant or 'harder to reach' needs.

Table 8.1 Stages of putting together a provision map

Audit needs: collect data on:
• Whole-school attainment results, year group patterns of need, highlighted problems
• Learners with Code of Practice graduated response and disability needs (SEND)
• Vulnerable groups: EAL, looked after, disadvantaged, travellers
• Other personalised needs
• Parents' and pupils' views

Map out provision:
• Compare audit data with current provision. Where are the gaps?
• Decide on criteria and parameters for provision map
• Match to funding streams (Ring-fenced and not? Needs versus resource?)
• Cost out provision for each learner and/or year group focus (pattern of need)
• Consult research on what works best; value for money?
• Check that individual SEND requirements and personalised needs are included
• For each learner: the starting point and expected achievement outcome

Organise efficient delivery:
• Train all staff in consistent approaches to intervention, teaching methods, timescales, entry/exit criteria, assessment and monitoring strategies
• Clarify roles and responsibilities
• Link together all three waves of intervention (QFT, provision, EHCPs)
• Involve parents and pupils in supporting delivery
• Link with external specialist involvement/advice

Individualise for annual and termly reviews:
• Decide how the provision map is to be individualised for parent/pupil confidentiality
• Clarify for all staff, which other documentation informs/contributes to the provision map: Learners' personal plans? QFT differentiation? Personalised approaches? Notes from parental conversations? Staff records?

Evaluate and update:
• Impact on each learner's progress: from starting point to expected outcome (distance travelled?)
• Each intervention: How well has each learner progressed on it? Value for money?
• Use annual and termly pupil reviews to update and refresh map as necessary
• Impact on key stage or year group results (patterns): from audit level to outcome
• What do outcomes point to? Further staff training or deployment? Change of intervention programmes? More intensive focus on parent/pupil involvement?
• Annual audit to plan next cycle
• Evaluate provision map itself: How well did it work? Format? Does it need rejigging?

Provision maps versus personal plans

For years schools have wrestled with the function and design of Individual Education Plans (IEPs). Some schools still use these but some don't, which is why I now call them 'personal plans'. What schools call IEPs no longer matters as the Code allows 'schools to determine their own ... record keeping' (6.72). Key questions:

• Where do personal plans fit with provision-mapping?
• What are the differences?
• Do pupils need both a provision map and a personal plan?

My view is that IEPs have not worked effectively for many reasons. They have:

• Often been isolated from other forms of intervention;
• Not been owned or understood by pupils and parents;
• Not been reinforced through QFT;
• Not been reinforced in other areas of the curriculum;
• Not always contained SMART targets (specific, measurable, achievable, relevant, timed);
• Often focused on literacy and numeracy only;
• Often neglected major barriers to learning (self-help, social and communication skills).

IEPs have been far from perfect, but can an individualised provision map perform the same function at termly and annual reviews? I believe so. Review targets are easily aligned with intervention entry and exit criteria, and the provision map includes *all* additional provision, not just isolated targets. An individualised provision map also involves learners and parents more extensively, through the entire breadth and depth of the intervention package. Might IEPs now be just another piece of paper to juggle with amongst piles of redundant paperwork?

Can an individualised provision map be SMART enough to subsume an IEP? Check:

- Specific: Yes, through the stated intervention outcomes and distance travelled;
- Measurable: Yes, through entry and exit criteria and measuring tools for success;
- Achievable: Yes, because the audit provides a starting point and expected outcomes;
- Relevant: Yes, because the map includes all audited needs relevant to the whole of the intervention strategy, not just part of it;
- Timed: Yes, because interventions are time-limited.

My view is not shared by all LAs; for example, Wiltshire Local Authority states that provision maps are not a *complete* replacement for IEP-style personal plans and are advising their schools to continue with IEPs (see www.wisenet.wiltshire.gov.uk). So what are schools to do? Much depends on the quality of the provision map. It is well worth spending time getting it right and ensuring that all staff follow the map together, without some deviating from the main track.

Where schools do decide to have both a provision map and a personal plan, both documents need to be linked so that all staff know exactly what their destination is (pupil outcomes), how they are to get there (collective strategies and intervention routes), and how effective the provision has been (pupil progress from starting point to destination).

Funding and costing provision maps

How do schools manage funding streams? Separately or together? Combined funding streams offer more coherent provision across the board that is streamlined and less conflicting. Funding should focus on outcomes rather than separate pots of money.

Additional provision may be resourced from:

- Element 1 (core): number of pupils in school. Some ATDF provision involves 'QFT tweaking' without extra cost;
- Element 2: notional SEN budget, from the LA formula, often worked out from low literacy/maths attainment and free school meals. If a school has more SEND than expected, there may be LA top-up. The notional budget should meet up to £6,000 of each SEN pupil's provision (at the time of writing);
- Element 3: top-up from the LA high needs block for EHCP or other high needs;
- Pupil premium: to reduce the attainment gap for disadvantaged learners.

Which parts of the budget are ring-fenced and which are for schools to make their own judgements? The Code (6.96–7) suggests that the notional budget, that is not ring-fenced, should provide high-quality support for the total SEND population. Schools need to take a strategic approach, using all available resources, including pupil premium. Schools are not expected to meet the costs of expensive provision from core funding (Code, 6.90).

The pupil premium (PP) is intended to narrow the achievement gap between disadvantaged (free school meals – FSM) and non-disadvantaged pupils. How might PP be spent? Again, much depends on what the provision-mapping audit has revealed. PP spending strategies include:

- Some learners in smaller class sizes
- More targeted individual support; for example, reading recovery
- Mentoring of selected students
- Home tutoring of pupils in maths or English
- Support for secondary coursework
- Family learning; teaching parents how to support basic skills
- Counselling for selected pupils and families
- School focus on language, literacy or maths.

The pupil premium can address whatever needs the provision map audit has revealed, from the perspective of disadvantage. To contribute to an OFSTED 'outstanding' judgement, a school's pupil premium spend should result in either disadvantaged pupils achieving the same levels as peers, or their achievement rising at a rapid rate. Some children from white, British, low-income families are likely to have SEND, so SEN support and pupil premium funding overlap is significant.

Given that less attention is often paid by schools to developing personal, social and independent skills, should some pupil premium spending be directed at these neglected areas, as they represent the qualitative (process) areas of learning that lead to the quantitative outcomes identified from provision-mapping?

Dunford (2013), in his role as pupil premium champion, informs us that the disadvantaged achievement gap widens significantly with age: from 16% (68% against 84%) at the end of Year 6, to 26% (40% against 66%) at GCSE (5 or more A–Cs). If accurate, do these figures suggest that progress for some disadvantaged pupils slows throughout secondary school? It would appear so. Cocco (2015) reports that the pupil premium appears to have had little effect on disadvantaged children in secondary schools. Dunford (2013) further reported that for the school year 2014–15, wider funding has been targeted at Year 7 summer schools and Year 7 literacy/numeracy catch-up. It remains to be seen what effect this has on the secondary achievement gap.

The clear message for SENCOs and other finance managers is that funding for additional provision-mapping needs to be:

- Targeted relentlessly at the needs and problems revealed by the audit;
- Linked to national achievement gap data (secondary schools to reduce the 26% gap);
- Evaluated as a value-for-money measure, through the progress of individual learners.

Structure and models for provision-mapping

There is no single model for a provision map because schools need to design and *own* what they create. The collective effort that members devote to making up their own provision map is itself a valuable training experience. From audit to evaluation, the whole school ends up knowing far more about itself as a teaching and learning organisation. Hopefully, the following section will help SENCOs to guide staff discussions.

How might the map be organised? What is the basic structure, around which other information is included? Is it organised by:

- Priority funding: 'must, should, could'?
- Key stage, year or class?
- The three-waves model?
- Code of Practice graduated response?
- Categories of SEN?
- The Code's four areas of need (interaction/communication; cognition/learning; social and emotional; sensory and physical)?
- Vulnerable categories, each matched to a funding stream?

However organised, the mapping should allow schools to evaluate provision in terms of: pupils receiving it; outcomes; costings; types of interventions; and most importantly, value for money. An effective provision map is not simply a list of interventions with no link to how each has contributed to pupil achievement.

The design may be led by what the audit has uncovered as whole-school patterns of need. If a particular key stage or year group has priority needs, the provision map might be designed around these, as a year-on-year response to changing patterns.

Alternatively, if the audit shows that waves of provision are not operating seamlessly, waves may lead the provision-mapping process. Mapping by waves may encourage greater pedagogical reflection over time. Including all three waves on one model might generate discussion about how they interact for each learner. A focus on waves may also clarify for parents what their child's combined intervention is.

Mapping by Code of Practice is more likely to mirror SEN systems and focus minds on how graduated responses work for each type of SEN, or each Code area of need.

The audit may indicate poor performance amongst particular vulnerable groups, in which case, should this lead the design? The map could show children in each group, as well as which interventions they receive, cost and outcomes.

Designing the provision map from whole-school issues highlighted by audit offers schools a direct link back, in order to evaluate data like-for-like. For example, if improving literacy in Year 3 is a major need, then organising part of the provision map around this directs evaluation back to the starting point.

How can the provision map be individualised? 'Leading on Inclusion' made clear that IEPs are not the only way to record individual provision (DfES 2005a). Confidentiality is an issue if the map covers year groups. How is individual data separated?

'Leading on Inclusion' also promoted the 'must, should, could' model. Table 8.2 outlines the rationale, and Table 8.3 offers a format, led by each priority, and organised for each year group.

Table 8.2 Rationale for 'must, should, could'

Must	Should	Could
Statutory and essential needs: • EHCPs • Equality Act reasonable adjustments	Pupils whose needs impact on both their own progress and those of others if not addressed • Behavioural • Personalised Pupils with the potential to catch up with average expectations	Pupils who would benefit if funding allows
Mainly Wave 3	Waves 2 and 3	Mainly Wave 1: additional provision but linked to QFT
• Response 4 of the Code • Pupil premium	• Pupils at Response 2/3 funded by SEN Support • Pupil premium	For example: • Additional TA in class • Group work • Pupil premium

Table 8.3 Format for the 'must, should, could' model

Year ...	Name	Wave 2 Literacy	Wave 3 Literacy	Wave 2 Maths	Wave 3 Maths	Speaking and listening	Social skills	Other
Must								
Should								
Could								

Reasons why the 'must, should, could' model works well include:

- Staff attention is focused on layers of need, starting with the most important;
- It prioritises SEND legislation by placing statutory requirements first (must);
- It matches funding streams and costings to each priority.

Table 8.4 illustrates a provision map based on the waves, while Table 8.5 shows how an individualised provision map could easily include personal plans (IEPs).

Table 8.4 Mapping by waves

Year group …	Speaking/ listening	Reading	Writing	Maths	Removing barriers	Personal -isation	Costs x numbers of pupils
Wave 1: Additional in class provision Code Response 1							14 pupils ? x ? = ?
Wave 2: Code Response 2 to 3							9 pupils
Wave 3: Code Response 3 to 4 (EHCPs)							6 pupils

Table 8.5 Including personal plans on individualised provision maps

Name: .... DOB .... SEN type/area of need................. Disability.................................... Vulnerable group..................... Year group....... Class.........	QFT differentiation (Wave 1): Language.............. Reading................. Writing/spelling................. Maths.................. Other..................
Wave 2 intervention/provision: .... Intervention details .... Cost...................... Achievement starting point........................ Achievement end point....................... Progress made.............................	Wave 3 intervention/provision: .... Intervention details........................... Cost...................... Achievement starting point............... Achievement end point................... Progress made.....................
Personal Plan: Autumn term Targets Strategies: who, what, when, where	Review date........... Notes from review meeting: whether targets achieved or not, any issues, next steps?
Personal Plan: Spring term Targets Strategies: who, what, when, where	Review date........... Notes from review meeting
Personal Plan: Summer term Targets Strategies: who, what, when, where	Review date............. Notes from review meeting
End-of-year pupil progress summary:	Next intervention cycle:

With reference to Table 8.5, details should include the following:

- Number of weeks
- Length of each session
- Frequency per week
- Timing
- Who delivers the intervention
- Staff/pupil ratio
- Costing
- Achievement: starting and finishing points, and progress made.

Without such information it is difficult for schools to match progress to value for money.

The effectiveness of the provision-mapping system depends on consistency, especially where different staff members deliver the same interventions. Guidelines, such as those shown in Table 8.6, help to ensure all staff deliver interventions in a similar way, and could be part of the staff training that precedes delivery. Such user information could be compiled over time and added to as new programmes join the intervention repertoire.

Table 8.6 User information for delivery of interventions

Name and type of provision	ELS? Paired reading? *Jolly Phonics?* Shared writing?
SEN focus/area of need Vulnerable group	Literacy? Cognition? Behaviour? Social? Travellers, looked after, EAL
Wave	Used as Wave 2 or Wave 3 provision?
Entry criteria/starting point	Eg. Pupils in Year 3 with Year 1 writing skills
Key stage or year group	Which whole-school audit issue is this intervention actioned towards: Year 6 low achievers in maths; Year 1 low achievers in phonics; boys reading in Year 2; language in reception?
Lead person	Who has main responsibility: SENCO, INCO, EAL co-ordinator?
Supported by	Perhaps an external agency? EP?
Start/end dates and timescale	12 weeks?
Frequency	15 minutes per day? 1 hour twice a week?
Delivered by	Names of TAs or other staff
Pupil grouping	Maximum of four in group? Six?
Cost	Cost of TA hours? Materials?
HOW TO DELIVER	Guidelines could include: • Basic principles for teaching this skill • Maintaining interest and motivation • Offering positive feedback to learners • How to observe/manage the intervention • How to link together each step of programme • How to summarise pupil outcomes
How to record pupil outcomes	What data to record, on what? In what format? Given to whom?
Method of evaluation	Reading test? Outcomes matched to pre-specified targets?
Exit criteria	Gain of six months in reading age?
Pupils receiving this intervention during this timescale	Pupils' names added each term

How each school designs a provision map reflects how its key players think, its styles of teaching and management, as well as what a particular audit reveals. It is never a good idea to copy the same model as neighbouring schools if their audits, staffing, pupil populations or ways of organisation are different. Provision maps need to suit the unique shape of each school.

Depending on what information they carry, provision maps can be complex documents, which is why many schools, especially larger ones, depend on ICT software to support the process. Support from 'Provision Map Writer' (www.capita-sims.co.uk) or from www.provisionmap.co.uk offer options for schools to design their own provision maps, but schools still have to make informed choices on the right format and content.

Evaluation

Evaluation should be annual. If schools have begun their mapping cycle from the start of a school year, using the previous year's achievements as the audited starting point, it makes sense to evaluate at the end of the school year, to plan the next.

Evaluation answers the following questions:

- Have pupils progressed as a result of provision? How far have expected outcomes been met? Have interventions been spread fairly to address needs?
- Does progress data indicate that funding has been well spent?
- Have outcomes dealt with the issues thrown up by the audit?
- What needs to change? Different intervention programmes? Different strategies?
- Has the provision-mapping itself been effective? What needs to change for the next annual cycle?

Who evaluates? Everyone involved in additional provision: all staff, external specialists, parents and pupils, as well as OFSTED. As consumers of the provision-mapping system, parents and pupils form the centre of feedback that helps to design provision for the following year.

How might external specialists contribute to the evaluation? If specialist advice, based on the audit, has contributed to intervention decision making, feedback is invaluable. For example, if the whole-school audit highlighted significant discipline issues, or bullying, perhaps in a year group, that needed a behaviour specialist, that specialist needs to be part of monitoring and evaluation. Similarly, if the Educational Psychologist (EP) has been involved in setting up personalised intervention for some 'hard to teach' learners, EP assessment of those learners should be included.

OFSTED needs evidence:

- That the school has involved all contributors in its evaluation;
- Of individual pupil's 'start and end' attainments/achievements and whether good progress has been made;
- That whole-school needs revealed by the audit have been tackled;
- That funding has been well spent.

Contributors bring their own perspectives to evaluation. Most parents are understandably more concerned with outcomes for their child. A class teacher is likely to want class-based results. TAs may be concerned with outcomes of interventions they have personally delivered. External specialists may be interested primarily in the part of the audit that involved them. OFSTED is highly likely to take a national view, being concerned with the achievements of vulnerable groups known to be currently under-performing.

What are SENCOs and other pupil managers more likely to be concerned with? Perhaps all of it, but especially the overall relationship between pupil progress and funding. SENCOs (with other managers) help to evaluate the provision map from a whole-school perspective, in terms of:

- Providing effective graduated responses for all at SEN Support or with an EHCP;
- Reasonable adjustments for disabled pupils;
- Vulnerable groups highlighted from the audit;
- Staffing: has training for the provision been adequate? What more needs to be done?
- Funding: how wisely has it been spent? Have all learners received a fair share?

Which areas of pupil progress need to be measured? Wave 2 structured interventions may have their own built-in success criteria for literacy or maths. They measure how far a pupil has moved along a skill-based programme. This type of measurement is often quantitative, supported by a range of standardised tests, reading ages or criterion-referenced skill comparisons between starting points and outcomes.

If an intervention has set out to improve well-being or other non-academic areas, perhaps in the form of highly personalised strategies, how would this be measured? From the outset, non-academic interventions should have start and end points for observers. Examples of qualitative evaluation include:

- A reduction in absence for a child who has been truanting;
- Increased involvement of parents for a child with behaviour difficulties;
- Improved interactive play for a child who has suffered bereavement;
- Elimination of bullying in a targeted year group;
- Evidence of improved independent learning;
- A turnaround in motivation from a pupil who has received daily mentoring.

Is there an inherent conflict between what schools desire most — quantitative outcomes measured through literacy and maths that improve overall results — and qualitative outcomes that learners need, in order to get them on board in the first place? Might the qualitative desires of some pupils help to steer outcomes towards the quantitative desires of whole-school success? Therefore, when evaluating how provision-mapping has worked out, is it worth considering how qualitative planning may be the process towards the quantitative end product?

Chapter summary

This chapter has brought together many thoughts and ideas from earlier chapters, and illustrated how the *process* of provision-mapping illustrated in Table 8.1 (from audit to evaluation) mirrors the Code's sequential stages of response (assess, plan, do, review). Each step of provision-mapping brings into play earlier principles, thoughts or concepts in the following ways:

- Audit (assess): SEN types and disabilities? Four areas of learning needs? Vulnerable, underachieving groups? Priority areas of school-based need?
- Map provision (plan): Code graduated responses, inclusion principles, QFT and the waves, knowledge gained about SEN from the IDP and AfA projects and personalised approaches;
- Organise delivery, and individualise (do): Select the best value-for-money resources, train staff to deliver interventions, synchronise with annual/termly reviews, monitor progress;
- Evaluate (review): Bring together all evidence to plan the next cycle.

Throughout this process, the task of SENCOs is surely to gather ongoing evidence to decide where their particular school is stronger or weaker. Provision-mapping enables those in management positions to work out which puzzle pieces are missing from the picture of whole-school and individual success. If evidence is noted as an ongoing feature, as delivery happens, final evaluation is likely to be less cumbersome and time-consuming.

At the end of the day, whole-school results depend on pupil outcomes. Where individuals achieve, the school also achieves!

Chapter 9

Reconsidering the school workforce

Provision-mapping relies on the workforce: people make systems work. How much effort do school managers put into ensuring that their particular workforce is not only trained for the job, but inspired by the feel-good factor, as well as the consequences of pupil outcomes?

This chapter considers:

- Taking stock of the school workforce
- The 'people' aspects of the SENCO role
- Changing habits, culture and practice
- Roles and responsibilities
- Managing additional adults
- Matching practice with policy.

Taking stock

If ambitious aspirations for SEND and other vulnerable learners are to be realised, the school workforce must rise to the challenge. Staffing in schools often evolves in a haphazard way as people leave or change working hours. A staffing review might question whether the current workforce is up to the job of delivering mapped provision, and pose questions such as:

- How well does our workforce match audited needs?
- What changes are needed in recruitment and deployment?
- What training is needed for teachers and TAs?

Taking stock of the learners may question:

- What has the provision-mapping audit revealed about learners? Are they attaining better or worse than national averages? Their stated aims and expectations?
- What does the school *pattern* of needs indicate (year/class groups), and how do 'must and should' funding priorities cut across these audited patterns?

Having matched data about learners to information about staffing, how well is the whole workforce geared up to deliver the provision map, and where are the gaps in skills and knowledge?

The SENCO role now

The responsibilities of SENCOs with regard to SEND (outlined in Chapter 2), reminds us that the SENCO role has shifted significantly from one who 'did' to one who now coordinates the collective 'doing'. Table 9.1

Table 9.1 The changed SENCO role

Traditional SENCO role	Expanded SENCO role
Identify learners with SEN, often using standardised tests	Identifying needs using a broader range of data SEN has become SEND (disabilities)
Teach some learners with SEN, often by withdrawing from class	More emphasis on management than teaching groups or individuals
Write SEN policy, with regard to the Code of Practice	Involve colleagues in writing whole school SEND policy Collaborate on other policies: inclusion, behaviour, well-being, vulnerable groups
Write IEPs, with help from class teachers	Provision-mapping taken over from IEPs? Collaborate with teachers *re* provision-mapping and personalisation strategies Support staff with personal plans at Wave 1
Organise, collate evidence for, and attend IEP reviews	Continued with more emphasis on parental contributions and provision-mapping outcomes Parents as equal partners in process
Organise LA evidence for statements and organise annual reviews	Statements now EHCPs, greater collaboration among school, health and social services Learners and parents at centre of process
Liaise with external specialists about individual children	Continued with greater emphasis on provision-mapping needs revealed by school audit
Informing classroom colleagues about what children with SEN need	Supporting classroom colleagues in situ Focus on QFT and waves Supporting pedagogical development Continued IDP teacher training on SEN
Liaising with parents/carers, informing them of additional provision	Parents and pupils leading provision
Rarely involving children in their goals/targets	Recognising pupil voice, giving learners choice of provision
Managing the Learning Support Assistants for children with SEN	Managing TAs at different levels: higher level teaching assistants (HLTAs) Wider network of TA tasks: waves and delivering interventions through provision-mapping
Reviewing progress for SEN, often by re-using standardised tests	Greater range of data for evaluation Regular tracking of pupil progress Cross-curricular evidence
Sometimes managing the budget for SEN	Continued, also working with colleagues to coordinate funding streams for all learners who need more than QFT

illustrates how the role has expanded and requires new skills. This section is about the *people* skills associated with the SENCO role.

While SENCOs may disagree with some points listed in Table 9.1, most would agree that their role has expanded. SENCOs now spend a greater proportion of time:

- Collaborating with colleagues;
- In conversations with parents;
- Involving external specialists in whole-school provision-mapping;
- Justifying the use of funding with other senior managers;
- Talking with learners about goals and aspirations.

This outward-looking role requires a greater repertoire of people skills than its traditional counterpart. It is far more difficult to influence change in others than it is to change one's own views and practices. Is the modern SENCO:

- A champion for SEND learners, promoting high aspirations and achievement?
- A change-agent influencing school culture and policy on behalf of vulnerable groups?
- An adviser observing and supporting improved classroom pedagogy?
- A manager of systems responding to Code of Practice and equality issues?
- A strategist, thinking ahead, rationalising, considering *how* to achieve outcomes?
- A manager of people organising and coordinating staff who deliver interventions?
- A trainer equipping the workforce with the required skills and knowledge?
- A researcher and resource-provider, gathering the best programmes and materials?
- A negotiator treading a fine line to satisfy parents and other stakeholders?
- A supporter of colleagues who fear change?
- A risk-taker often trying personalised strategies that are 'off the wall'?

The modern SENCO role involves a number of very different subroles. To make things happen, SENCOs need to make their voices heard. They need to be movers and shakers!

SENCOs as whole-school movers and shakers

What does the provision-mapping audit highlight as a need for change? Does it confirm what SENCOs already know? Colleagues may see impending change as threatening. The word 'change' suggests something new and different, threatening to uproot what, for some, has long been familiar, even comforting in its 'sameness'.

So, for colleagues to go on a 'change journey' they need to feel motivated and energised, without fear of consequences should their part in the changes involve temporary snags or problems. Any initial stumbling blocks need to be regarded as further challenges, with outcomes borne by the many, not the few. Change is more likely to be supported by a no-blame culture. Colleagues need to know:

- Why the change is necessary: clear, compelling evidence from the audit;
- What needs to happen, who is involved, how: the process, timescale, methods;
- How they will be supported and guided at every step of the journey;
- At the end of the change journey: what is in it for them, as well as the school.

All staff need to feel successful so the more individual motivation that SENCOs stir into the new mix, the more likely changes will happen. SENCOs need to start slowly, using colleagues already tuned in as key players to spread the word and set positive examples. Remember my anecdote about ex-grammar school staff needing to face their fears about the new comprehensive intake? I worked with the History staff first because the new head of department was anxious to set the scene and make his mark.

'Moving and shaking' colleagues who have been set in their ways needs all the persuasive skills a SENCO possesses, as well as a host of interpersonal qualities, such as:

- Sensitivity when faced with barriers, difficult staff or parent situations;
- The ability to 'read' people: know when to nudge and when to back off;
- Flexibility to problem-solve and respond to different challenges;
- Patience: colleagues need to move at their own pace;
- Confidence in the anticipated outcomes.

Resistance to change may explain why, in spite of numerous documents, resources and training made available to schools, the achievement gap is still wider than it should be. Depending on the audit, the process of provision-mapping is likely to send some shock waves through the staffroom. Handling them may need a bit of SENCO muscle.

SENCOs as managers of relationships

Joint working strengthens the potential for change through a consistent approach to collecting audit data, identifying needs, mapping provision and influencing improvements in classroom pedagogy. Figure 9.1 illustrates the tricky balance of SENCO professional relationships. Why tricky? Reaching out to people who we are managed by, as effectively as we reach out to those we are either on a par with, or are managed by us, is often difficult, especially if we are trying to get them all on board and paddling in the same direction.

SENCOs need from heads:

- Time: to work with other staff, converse with parents and pupils, observe classrooms, model good practice, liaise with external specialists, conduct reviews thoroughly by involving parents and learners;
- Status: to drive change forward;
- Opportunities for training: to keep up with SEND and relevant developments;
- Knowledge of, and access to, budgets;
- Support for risk-taking: change needs risks!

While solid, well-thought-out systems are essential for success, relationships are equally important. SENCOs need to know that a head stands behind them if things go pear-shaped.

Working with teacher colleagues may require SENCOs to:

- Use sensitive coaching techniques;
- Observe lessons within an atmosphere of mutual trust;
- Provide new resources for teachers to try, and give feedback;
- Share successes and failures to encourage teachers to venture from familiar to new.

What about external specialists? They support SENCOs in different ways; for example:

- Consultation and advice on whole-school issues;
- Assessment and advice on individual pupils;
- Training on areas of SEN for teachers and/or TAs.

Many external services are now 'bought in', so SENCOs need to be clear how much of the budget is used for external support and for what purpose. How far are specialists involved in provision-mapping, and what proportion of the overall budget is needed for external input?

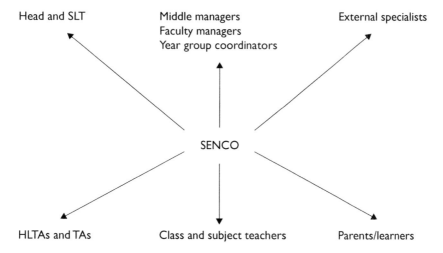

Figure 9.1 Balancing SENCO professional relationships

Governors need training too as they play a key role in policy development and the provision-mapping cycle. The relationship between SENCO and SEN governor is crucial.

Parents do much more than influence additional provision. The new Code makes clear that parents must be equal partners, so is the SENCO/parent relationship one of mutual information-giving and decision-making? Is there a fluid and open-ended two-way process towards individualised provision-mapping?

Last, but certainly not least, the learners. I perceive relationships with learners undergoing the greatest change. No longer are teaching and learning on alternative sides of the coin; they stand together, each supporting the other through:

- Respectful sharing of viewpoints and opinions;
- Opportunities for pupils to shape learning through personalisation;
- Self-responsibility and independence.

Learning that is done *with,* and not *to,* ceases to be a one-way channel of communication. Young learners are now growing up with greater confidence to challenge and interrogate what they receive, and take responsibility for their understanding. Learning is active, not passive. Learning that informs teaching demonstrates a reversal of the traditional pupil/teacher relationship, and could generate greater respect from learners as their views are seen to influence change.

Within these changing relationships SENCOs (and class teachers) often select intuitively from a range of interpersonal skills they may be hardly aware they possess.

Managing the training and deployment of additional adults

Learner outcomes from the provision-mapping cycle often depend on how effectively TAs deliver interventions. Their training list may be longer than we think. Table 9.2 has some suggestions, as a starting point for thinking about TA professional development. Larger or smaller schools may view these areas differently, but the training/support of teaching assistants must match up to provision-mapping demands.

A report on the deployment of support staff (DfES 2006a) concluded that the impact on learners' achievement could be improved if:

- Job descriptions are clear and up to date;
- Deployment is better matched to audited provision-mapping needs;
- Time for liaison is included in TA contracted hours;
- Training is better directed to the tasks that TAs perform;
- Appraisals are done annually.

Amongst the comments was the view that support staff benefit teaching by allowing teachers more time with non-SEND learners (DfES 2006a, p. 16). Since the mushrooming of supporting adults in classrooms (numbers have roughly trebled since about 2000), many SEND pupils have received less focused time from teachers. Children with SEND have the same entitlement to be taught by teachers, but many are being trained indirectly to rely on additional adults, resulting in a huge loss of independence and self-coping abilities.

Blatchford *et al.* (2015) report similar issues that schools now need to deal with, and make recommendations; namely that Teaching Assistants:

- Should not be an informal teaching resource for low-attaining pupils;
- Should add value to what teachers do, not replace them;
- Should help learners to develop independence and self-manage their learning;
- Must be fully prepared for their roles;

Table 9.2 What Teaching Assistants need

Level of provision	Know	Do	Understand
Wave 1: To support QFT and teachers' lesson planning	How: • Different teachers teach • Different children learn • Lessons are adapted • Personalisation arrangements • Disability adjustments	Apply policies: • SEND, inclusion, discipline and behaviour, health/safety, safeguarding • Maintain records of learning • Be consistent with teaching methods	• Pedagogy of learning and progression • How to further adapt work as needs arise • Some areas of SEN and pupils' needs
Wave 2/3: SEN Support and disability	As above, plus how to: • Deliver interventions • Work with groups • Operate ICT programmes • Support personal plans	As above, plus: • Organise provision • Maintain records for reviews • Manage group dynamics and behaviour	As above, plus: • Progression in basic skills • Basic psychology of behaviour • When learning has, or has not happened
Wave 3: SEN Support and EHCPs	As above, plus how to: • Deliver individual interventions • Record outcomes • How to support 'hard to teach' pupils • Requirements of EHCPs	As above, plus: • Manage resources • Maintain records for annual and termly reviews	• How individual teaching works • How different individuals learn best (styles) • Small-step targets (P scales; performance indicators for value-added target-setting – PIVATS), how to recognise progress in small steps

• Should be used to deliver high quality, evidence-based interventions; impact is high;
• Should ensure explicit connections between QFT and structured interventions.

The report also suggests that the effect of TAs on pupil achievement has been minimal, as TAs have mainly supported pupils with the greatest needs, who have made the least progress. The report does not criticise TAs, but does suggest that managers need to rethink TA roles and training. These recommendations offer a starting point.

A further element of rethinking the TA role involves purpose. Is the purpose of TA support to:

• Ensure pupils complete tasks, or develop understanding of ideas and concepts? I suggest the latter.
• Should TAs focus on process or product? Surely the former.

Following the rethink of how TAs need to be deployed, and their express purpose as 'support staff', what should their training comprise? Training for TAs has traditionally been offered by the (former) Training and Development Agency (2009a), in the form of National Occupational Standards for TAs, covering a diverse range: pastoral, bilingual, behaviour, safeguarding, observing and reporting, positive relationships, literacy, numeracy, ICT and SEN support generally. These standards have also linked in with accredited training for higher level teaching assistants (HLTAs).

Standardised training offers a secure grounding for the job and provides a certificate of basic competence, but it does not equip support staff to deliver specific provision-mapping interventions. Therefore TAs need:

• Basic standardised training: the foundations of what they are required to know, do or understand that support their role in *any* school;
• Specific training that conforms to the school's provision-mapping, policies and procedures.

From my own observations, and those of the above-cited report, TA training has often not been directed to the tasks support staff actually perform. Time is always an issue, but the end result of not making sure that TAs are trained in the *specifics* could be failure to achieve provision-mapping outcomes. TAs must also be able to apply whole-school policies to their practice. Consistency is essential to success.

Recommendation 5 of the Lamb Inquiry was for the guidance on deploying teaching assistants to be developed (DCSF 2009e). This has now been done (Blatchford *et al.* 2015). The skills and knowledge of support staff need to be better harnessed if SEND goals are to be achieved. The DfE is now developing new TA professional standards.

What else might support staff need? Ongoing feedback on the job? Support for when things go wrong? Someone to ask advice from 'as and when', not just at meetings? All of these. In larger schools, HLTAs can help SENCOs to develop a strong TA team.

The success of provision-mapping often lies in the capable hands of support staff, whose 'hands-on' role may bring them closer than teachers to the SEND learners, whose outcomes inform evaluation. So, for support staff, TLC is an investment.

It is also worth considering that between 90% and 95% of the budget is spent on human resources. Those resources must be seen to represent value for money!

So far we have considered the SENCO role in relation to managing others, or being managed. But SENCOs have needs too.

What do SENCOs need?

The framework was set up to help SENCOs perform their role in accordance with the Code (Training and Development Agency 2009b). The learning outcomes centred around:

- Statutory and significant SEND developments (Code of Practice and Equality);
- The participation and achievements of SEND learners;
- Key policies relating to SEND;
- Working strategically with school colleagues and governors;
- Deploying support staff;
- Working in partnership with external professionals;
- Budget management: ensuring that funding is well spent;
- Strategies for improving outcomes for SEND learners;
- Coordinating additional provision, as provision-mapping;
- Leading, supporting and developing colleagues;
- Engaging with parents and carers.

Basic SENCO training seeks to raise 'skills, knowledge and understanding' that will narrow the achievement gap. Lamb (DCSF 2009e) made the following recommendations for the TDA to develop:

- Materials to support training at advanced level in the five main areas of SEN (Recommendation 6);
- Teachers with specialist skills in SEN and disability across clusters of schools (Recommendation 7).

Following the Lamb Inquiry's recommendations, advanced training materials have been developed for ASD, MLD, BESD (SEMH), SLCN and SpLD and dyslexia, these being areas of SEND that represent higher incidence in most mainstream schools. The first nine units cover general, good practice:

- Leadership and inclusion
- Definitions and data about SEND
- Theories of learning
- Coaching and mentoring
- Working with parents
- Lesson study.

Moore (2015) points to a move away from centralised SENCO training, and asks how the quality of the award will be protected, now that schools have to self-fund accredited SENCO training (central funding ceased in 2014). Providers have greater freedom to develop, validate and deliver training programmes that respond to the needs of schools, within the rubric of nationally agreed learning outcomes. The National Association for Special Educational Needs (NASEN) has taken on a facilitating role and includes quality SENCO trainers on their website for quality assurance.

There has been extended enthusiasm for developing SEND expertise from amongst class teachers. Does this mean that 'all teachers are teachers of SEN' is finally becoming rooted in practice? Does this also strengthen the shared approach to meeting SEND needs? The spread of SEND expertise should enhance QFT effectiveness as part of the waves approach to narrowing the achievement gap.

What do SENCOs need to effect change, and where do their skills and knowledge stem from? Table 9.3 poses some suggestions.

While much of what SENCOs need stems from generalised training, supplemented by national and Local Authority updates, much more comes from in-school observation and communication with colleagues, parents and pupils. Generalised courses form the foundations of knowledge and understanding, but 'walking the job' places such training in its specific context.

Research suggests that secondary schools have a wider achievement gap than primary. Should SENCOs therefore observe SEND learners in subject-based classrooms? I think so, because that is where reinforcement of English and Maths happens, and subject lessons take up the major proportion of learners' time. 'Walking the job' across subject-based classrooms, in liaison with teachers, informs the evidence base for secondary auditing and provision-mapping. Collaborative research between SENCOs and subject colleagues will narrow the secondary achievement gap.

Research from Szwed (2007) reported much diversity within the SENCO role. Some SENCOs are full-time class teachers, while others coordinate subjects, especially in smaller schools. Some SENCOs have dedicated time, while others have almost none. Under these circumstances, it is no surprise that SEND achievement, even between schools with similar SEND populations, varies considerably. Where SENCOs are allocated time to perform all aspects of their role, outcomes are bound to be more positive. Policy-making,

Table 9.3 The SENCO tool box

Have	Know	Do	Understand
• Status as member of senior leadership team • Back up from head • Clear vision and strength of purpose • Clear, transparent job description • Credibility from gained knowledge and experience • Time to meet and collaborate effectively	• All budgets that impact on SEND learners • About areas of SEN and disability • Code of Practice requirements • Equality legislation • How the school compares with national data • All policies that impact on SEND learners	• Involve staff, parents and learners in policy-making and SEND system • Lead collaborative provision-mapping cycle (assess, plan, do, review) • Observe SEND learners in QFT • Audit achievement and compare with national data • Train/support SEND workforce • Deploy support staff • Plan/chair annual and termly reviews • Have more in-depth conversations with parents and learners • Gather evidence and use strategically • Liaise with, and report to governors	• The dynamics of strategic and collaborative working • Steps of progression in language, literacy and numeracy • The school's main strengths and weaknesses • What class teachers need • What learners need • What parents need

provision-mapping, and all the other tasks that SENCOs undertake reflect the strengths and weaknesses of their own school systems and workforce.

Practice and policy

How closely does SEND practice reflect policy, and vice versa? The Code makes clear that governing bodies and heads take responsibility, while SENCOs, alongside other staff, take leading roles in strategic development and day-to-day operation.

How does SEND policy sit within the broader policy for inclusion? Many policies overlap: assessment, discipline and behaviour, record-keeping, safeguarding, health and safety. Policies are simply a means by which all staff know what they are meant to be doing. So, any written procedures that clarify whole-school direction represent policies, as does provision-mapping.

The Lamb Inquiry recommended that policy-making should be simplified, reflect updated practice and that parents and pupils should form a key part (DCSF 2009e): all staff need to be behind the policy and know where their role is in relation to it. In simple terms, policies contain:

- Agreed beliefs, values, aims, principles, purpose or functions that underpin practice;
- The who, what, when, where and how of implementation or delivery;
- The who, what, when, where and how of its evaluation.

Simply worded policies that are clear, concise and without unnecessary frills are more likely to be adhered to, and applied in context by all staff.

Chapter summary

This chapter has focused on the importance of teamwork, with people striving together towards agreed outcomes. No longer is the achievement of SEND learners a matter for SENCOs alone, or for secondary learning support departments working separately from subject-based colleagues.

I believe that when we concentrate on people systems almost take care of themselves. Schools with the best SEND outcomes almost certainly have a tightly-knit culture of 'we're all in this together'. So, spending time and effort on the skills, knowledge and overall efficiency of the workforce should be a major part of the SENCO role.

Chapter 10

Developing a SEND-friendly learning environment

'Narrowing the Gaps' highlighted QFT as the key to progress in *every subject,* even though its guidance was intended for literacy subject leaders (DCSF 2010d). Those whose job it is to observe QFT judge it mainly from the teaching side. From the pupils' perspective, QFT is their natural learning environment across the curriculum. So how effectively does it work for all learners, especially those who struggle to achieve? This chapter explores the 'Q' in QFT for learners with SEND.

What comprises an effective learning environment?

'Narrowing the Gaps' describes some characteristics of QFT that support all vulnerable groups, including those with SEND. These include:

- Focused lesson design with clear objectives;
- High levels of pupil engagement;
- High levels of interaction;
- Modelling and explanation;
- Emphasis on learning through talk;
- Expectations of self-responsibility and independence;
- Authentic praise.

The above needs are common to all learners. Just as all teachers are teachers of SEND, so every teacher is also a teacher of literacy (including foreign languages), as all subjects are taught through the medium of English.

The emphasis on learning through talk reminds us that learning in every subject revolves around different forms of speaking and listening: debate, explanation, question and answer. Building a friendly learning environment for all starts with talk.

Raised attainment for SEND learners is rooted in *every* classroom experience, not just in language, literacy and maths. The QFT of every subject contributes to pupils' overall *evaluation* of their school experience. If children with SEND were asked: 'What could we change to help you enjoy your learning and achieve your best?' responses might include:

- I want to learn without noise.
- Can we learn fewer spellings?
- I don't want to write.
- I want to work on my own.
- I need to lip-read but it's hard when the teacher turns round.
- I want to please myself what I do.
- I want to draw pictures.
- Can we talk more?

- I want to work with my friends more.
- Help me to remember things better.
- I don't like working by myself on the computer.
- I don't like reading aloud.

Even the best QFT cannot please all pupils all of the time. Whilst teachers try to offer all learners what they need, what they *want* may be different altogether. Nor can learners ever be given *all* their own way. However, personalisation invites schools to consider how to inject greater choice and freedom into learning without losing discipline and control.

Interaction and engagement stem from motivation, so:

- If some reluctant readers (often boys) prefer non-fiction, might choice stimulate interest?
- Do all children have to write about the same topic?
- Do all learners have to sit at the same table each lesson?
- Do all children have to learn through ICT? Could they sometimes work with an adult?
- Could children who struggle with, or hate writing, sometimes record work differently?
- Do all children have to rewrite edited work as neat copies?
- Could there be choice in the order of tasks?
- Could choice be through learning styles: write, draw or talk about a curricular topic?
- Could more children choose when to have adult support? Self-manage their needs?
- Would fewer, more targeted spellings inspire more children to learn them?

Personalised choices offer a means of motivating children who struggle in literacy and numeracy, but motivation is also greatly affected by how learners *feel*. For example:

- A child suffering from a divorce knows that adults make allowances for bad days;
- Children with autism know that peers will not think it odd when they sit by themselves because there has been class discussion about different ways of learning;
- Pupils with SLD are helped by peers, as well as adults, to do their best;
- A child with SLCN has confidence to ask for explanation without feeling embarrassed;
- Pupils with dyslexia are confident to attempt spellings, knowing they are always 'partly right', because the class has discussed 'trial and error' and sensitive responses;
- A child with moderate learning difficulties has trust and confidence to ask a friend for help as the class has discussed the values of helping each other;
- The child with SEMH knows the boundaries of classroom discipline and what happens when they are breached, as the class has had a discussion on classroom rules.

Do the above points suggest that a SEND-friendly learning environment develops as much from learners as from adults? It should! Learning needs to shape teaching. Talking about learning may help all pupils to regard their classroom as a special place where friends regularly do different things and learn in different ways.

In addition, non-SEND learners will behave with greater sensitivity towards SEND peers when they understand some of the challenges their struggling friends face, and are therefore more inclined to pitch in and help make their classroom a happy and positive learning environment for all. Classrooms belong to learners.

Observing and identifying fully inclusive learning

How do we know whether a classroom is fully inclusive and therefore SEND-friendly? Observing what goes on in classrooms across the curriculum is vital. Who observes whom? As well as leaders 'walking their job' throughout the school, could teachers observe each other? Classroom observation provides evidence of:

- Staff skills and knowledge: QFT differentiation/personalisation, reasonable adjustments and Wave 1 intervention;
- Embedding of good pedagogical practice;
- How learners appear to feel and respond.

The third point is particularly important if we are looking at classrooms from the perspective of learners rather than teachers. Fully inclusive classrooms will be full of pupils who are busy, engaged and interacting with someone, or something. Learning can be seen to lead teaching.

Classroom observation should be mutually agreed and focus on issues highlighted by the provision-mapping audit, for instance: SEMH; Year 8 boys' attainment; ASD achievement; writing in Year 2; achievement of children with sensory/physical difficulties; specific learning difficulties. Within this sensitive context, observers need to know *what* they are looking for and *why*.

Table 10.1 refers to the degrees of outcome (from Table 4.3) that should occur for SEND learners in mainstream. Do these degrees of outcome offer a focus for purposeful QFT observation? Table 10.1 is a starting point for staff to develop their own focused, outcome-based lesson observations.

Mindful of the challenges, how reasonable is it for *every* learner to gain skills and understanding 100% of the time? Is it more realistic for all children to emerge somewhere along the continuum (from engagement to skills and understanding)? Teachers may need reassurance that consistent perfection is unlikely, as teaching is a constantly changing mix of teaching/learning dynamics.

Having identified degrees of outcome for various learners, in relation to the focus of the observation, are there any *patterns*? Does a particular type, group or individual stand out as being taught more or less inclusively than others? Is there a particular reason?

Teachers are so busy they may miss 'invisible' children, who are neither disruptive nor actively involved. Some learners:

- Sit passively, hardly engaged;
- Look as if they are participating but produce little;
- Participate, but produce work that is not their best;
- Produce work either copied or derived from others.

External specialists often comment on the difference between classroom outcomes and what children demonstrate during individual assessment: many children reveal during specialist assessment, skills they do not use *independently* in class. Maybe focused observation can provide answers.

Table 10.1 Observing degrees of outcome at Wave 1

Lesson objectives:	Tasks and activities for each part: what are the selected learners doing?	Degrees of learning for each part: Engagement? Participation? Involvement? Gaining skills and understanding?	Notes and agreed action to improve learner outcomes
Introduction Main part of lesson Plenary/conclusion			

The iceberg factors

Barriers to learning are often far removed from what teachers observe, as shown in Figure 10.1. SENCOs and class teachers, sometimes with the help of external specialists, need to dive below the waterline to discover (and uncover) barriers that are not immediately obvious.

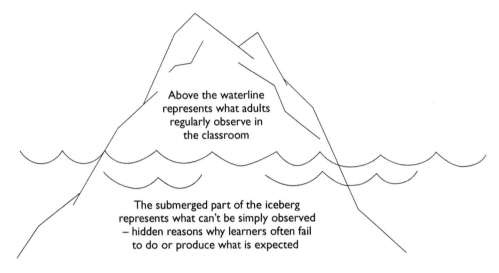

Figure 10.1 Iceberg factors

SENCOs need to ask:

- What is being observed in class?
- What might the learning barrier signify?
- Whose help do we need to identify the barriers and advise us?
- How does it relate to each of the Code's four areas of classroom need?

The following subsections identify hidden barriers, with some solutions.

Specific literacy difficulties: Possible dyslexia?

A. Classroom observation may show that a child:

- Cannot grasp or retain phonic knowledge;
- Has poor letter formation; reverses letters in words;
- Is delayed with spelling and struggles to write sentences;
- Loses control when writing longer pieces;
- Rarely finishes work;
- Produces very little literacy work, or work is very messy.

B. Iceberg barriers may include:

- Poor auditory memory;
- Slow processing of information affecting listening and reading;
- Poor phonological awareness: how sounds (phonemes) match letters/groups of letters (graphemes) to make words. Figure 10.2 illustrates the complexity of breaking down spoken language into words, then into the smallest units of sound (phonemes);
- Poor sequencing skills.

Spoken language: listeners have to separate it into parts
Paragraphs: containing categorised ideas
Sentences: from simple (could be one word!) to compound and complex
Phrases: meaning-carrying groups of words within each sentence
Words: short and long (from 'a' to 'antivivisectionism')
Syllables: parts of words 'antivivisectionism' has seven syllables
Phonemes: sounds; the smallest units of spoken language (*cat* and *chip* each have three sounds)

Figure 10.2 From spoken language to phonemes

C. Strategies to deal with hidden barriers may include:

- Stimulating poor memory, or teaching pupils how to compensate;
- Extra time for children to respond to oral work or complete writing;
- Revisiting previously taught phonics regularly;
- Transferring phonics across the curriculum; finding examples of phonic patterns;
- Sequencing: pictures in order of events, words to make sentences, number patterns;
- A multi-sensory approach to literacy: auditory, visual and kinaesthetic.

Possible Autism

A. Difficulties observed in class:

- Unable to join in discussion;
- Struggles to work with peers;
- Meltdown when routines are changed;
- Does not respond well to choices;
- Appears aggressive to other children or adults;
- Not conforming to classroom rules or routines.

B. Iceberg barriers may include:

- Problems with social interaction: child prefers to work alone;
- Child feels insecure: safety and security undermined by change;
- Not 'reading' actions of others and not understanding consequences of own actions;
- Not understanding emotions.

C. The autism-friendly classroom could:

- Teach explicitly how to 'be' in different social situations, perhaps using social stories;
- Introduce new routines carefully, with advanced notice and reassurance;
- Provide an individual workstation sometimes;
- Provide visual timetable for what happens, when, where, with whom (security feelings).

Speech, language and communication (SLCN):

A. Observations may include:

- Cannot explain problems
- Cannot use sentences
- Struggles to match appropriate words to intended meanings
- Does not follow instructions
- Unclear speech.

B. Iceberg barriers may be:

- Poor vocabulary
- Difficulties in processing receptive language
- Difficulties in expressing themselves.

C. Addressing SLCN barriers include:

- Pre-teaching vocabulary for reading schemes;
- Teaching subject-based vocabulary;
- Adults simplifying instructions, or verbally emphasising main meaning-carrying words (example, verbs);
- Teaching what a sentence is and modelling different types;
- Teaching how to manipulate words into different meanings: more in-depth extension of class-based work on grammar and syntax;
- Reference to the Speech and Language Service.

Cognitive learning difficulties (SLD or MLD)

A. Children with cognitive difficulties often demonstrate a range of problems:

- Unfinished work
- Inability to work without an adult
- Inability to follow instructions
- Failure to generalise skills and knowledge
- Limited ability to work out problems and puzzles: lack of reasoning and thinking skills
- Lack of retention
- General slowness across the curriculum.

B. Barriers may include those already mentioned, plus:

- Limited development of obscure concepts, due to lack of cognitive reasoning;
- Difficulties with reading comprehension (described in following textbox);
- Inability to grasp new ideas and connections between ideas.

C. Learners with cognitive difficulties benefit from previously mentioned ideas, plus:

- Concrete experiences: make learning practical, hands-on and visual;
- Multi-sensory activities: visual, auditory, kinaesthetic and social (VAKS);
- Small steps of learning, carefully built up;
- Explicit transfer of skills into other contexts;
- Explicit use of language;
- Meta-cognition: how to learn.

The complexities of comprehension

Aspects of reading, according to text type and reading purpose

As skilled readers we may not realise HOW we read. Depending on our purpose, we respond to different types of texts in different ways, using different skills:

- Searching for details: who, what, when, where, how and why.
- Summarising main idea: context, type, purpose, title. What the text is mainly about.
- Sequence: the order of events or parts of a task, in a story or set of instructions.
- Cause and effect: what caused something to happen and the consequences of it.
- Comparison: comparing people, places or things against others.

All texts contain these aspects of comprehension. As readers, we interpret each text according to its type and our purpose for reading it.

Depth of comprehension

Each of the above aspects can be understood at different levels of understanding:

- Literal: what is explicitly stated; reading the lines only.
- Inferential: what is implicit, between the lines, more thinking required.
- Re-organisational: the ability to reshape the text; to change tense, viewpoint, requiring good understanding of grammar and syntax.
- Evaluative: bringing our own experience to the text, in order to judge it, reflect on its merit or importance, or to consider the credibility of an argument.

The comprehension box

Imagine a Rubik's Cube, three-dimensional with breadth and depth. Its parts change to form different patterns. Similarly, reading different parts of texts changes our thinking patterns throughout the process. I think of this as a box with different aspects reaching down through each layer of understanding. According to their purpose, good readers dig deeply, below literal level, rummage about in the box and search for hidden meanings at deeper levels: from inferential, to re-organisational, to evaluative.

LEVEL OF COMPREHENSION	ASPECTS OF COMPREHENSION: details, main idea, sequence, cause/effect, comparison
LITERAL	Understanding only the lines: explicit
INFERENTIAL	Understanding between the lines: implicit
RE-ORGANISATIONAL	Able to reshape texts: with same meaning
EVALUATIVE	Using personal experience to judge/reflect

Different aspects float around within texts. A paragraph of comparison may be followed by one of cause and effect, to be followed by one on sequence. Skilled readers follow these changing parts and adapt their focus. Cue words often trigger comprehension responses. For example: 'because' for cause/effect; 'next' for sequence; or 'different' for comparison. The outcome is that reading comprehension is fully three-dimensional and highly effective.

Social, emotional and mental health (SEMH)

A. The challenges presented by SEMH are obvious to all teachers and support staff, often through low-level disruption, refusal to do tasks, and/or aggression. Beneath observed behaviours lurk many possible causes, often not identified owing to the dominating priority of the behaviour. Challenging behaviours may mask:

- Other types of learning difficulty: autism or dyslexia;
- Language problems: not knowing how to communicate;
- Significant cognitive difficulties;
- School social life conflicts with home circumstances;
- A significant but temporary emotional barrier (bereavement, parent in prison);
- Significant emotional barrier that needs professional help.

B. What is hidden below the surface of the behaviours (iceberg factors)? SENCOs need to check whether challenging behaviours are the cause or consequence of other learning difficulties. The same behaviours may have vastly different sources. Not all challenging behaviours arise from a SEND cause, but most do. So is the child-to-teacher message:

- I can't do what you ask because my learning difficulty is preventing me?
- I can't get it right because you are not clear what I need to do?
- I don't care: I want to do as I please?
- I can't concentrate on school work, so I play up. I need to talk about my emotional problem?

C. Solutions? Most learners want to conform and get on well with peers and adults in the classroom, so identifying the cause is a priority, however much staff need to deal urgently with the behaviour itself. Strategies to try:

- Make classroom routines and school discipline clear to the whole class: do a lesson on them (could be a talking or writing exercise);
- Ensure clear sanctions and rewards in equal measure;
- Ensure that all staff deal consistently with challenging behaviours;
- Take extra care when behaviour strategies are also disability 'reasonable adjustments' under the Equality Act;
- Be explicit when giving out instructions: could be written as well as verbal;
- Sometimes, offering a disruptive child extra responsibility works well;
- Tease out and celebrate strengths, rather than picking out recurring weaknesses; try to rebuild lost self-esteem;
- Put well-being at the top of the behaviour agenda: dig deep to find causes and demonstrate to the child that staff care about the person hidden inside the behaviour;
- Work with the home to apply strategies: where school and home are in conflict, few strategies can be effective in turning challenging behaviour around;
- Provide a mentor in school, or refer to external specialists (for example, CAMHS) to help deal with deep-seated emotional problems.

The above subsections represent the five areas of SEN for which the Lamb Inquiry recommended advanced training. Who needs to undertake such training? SENCO or class teachers? So that all schools reap the benefits, should clusters get together to spread expertise? It is for schools to decide.

Two more areas of specific learning difficulty deserve attention: dyspraxia (Developmental Coordination Disorder) and dyscalculia.

Developmental Coordination Disorder

Observed difficulties include: cutting, threading, forming letters, throwing/catching, running/jumping, general clumsiness and tendency to lose balance or fall over. PE teachers often notice problems with different movements.

These barriers separate into:

- Gross motor skills: running, jumping, catching, swinging on or climbing ropes;
- Fine motor skills, associated with hand and finger movements.

From the EYFS onwards, it is important to monitor difficulties in both areas, as these types of difficulties often need the support of a physiotherapist or occupational therapist.

Strategies to address dyspraxia include:

- Use of a computer if handwriting is a significant problem;
- Special pencil grips: experiment with different styles to find the right one;
- Focused practice in identified areas of difficulty;
- Additional time to perform movements and drawing: in PE, art or design and technology or other areas of learning where shape and space are involved.

Dyscalculia

This is often the mathematical version of dyslexia. If learners, in spite of much intervention with number work, still fail to grasp numerical relationships, dyscalculia should be investigated. Strategies include:

- Use of multi-sensory approaches for number work: making connections between senses;
- Use of visual apparatus to learn mathematical concepts;
- Practical approaches: linking number work to 'real' maths;
- Much reinforcement, consolidation and practised use of numbers in other areas of learning at each numerical stage before being moved to new levels.

Some strategies for addressing the main five areas of SEN apply also to non-SEN. We have seen that SEN represents a continuum, from mild, to moderate, through to severe, with many more children without SEN at the *mild end of the same type of difficulty*. For example, of all children who struggle with reading/spelling, very few have dyslexia. Is it worth exploring the benefits of all these strategies to support QFT for all? I think it is.

Iceberg factors apply far less to pupils with sensory and physical difficulties, as these are likely to have been identified early. Schools do, however, need the support of specialist services to determine the precise nature and extent of these disabilities, from the perspective of health and safety, as well as learning.

Not only do iceberg factors overlap, it is too easy to rely on surface evidence alone. Combining QFT and additional provision for all learners requires knowing them, inside and out. Classroom observation needs to trigger a process of drilling down with parents, to find submerged causes of pupils' difficulties. Only then can schools be confident that they know enough to teach them all effectively.

Resourcing SEND-friendly classrooms

Resources are the tools for teaching. It may seem obvious, but it is worth thinking about the range of resources available for the learners that teachers have spent much time getting to know.

The IDP materials offer a wealth of strategies to support QFT as an ongoing process of development: a starting point. But only schools know which resources suit the particular learning styles and needs of their audited learner population.

Many publishers target materials specifically for SEND. Whilst teachers need to match resources to types of difficulties, care must be taken to ensure that materials work for individuals. ICT is not always the answer. An ICT programme cannot answer a child's questions, nor can ICT deal with problems as they arise. For some vulnerable learners, the chance to talk is priceless!

SEND Gateway (see website) is an online partnership including the Department for Education, publishers, schools and voluntary organisations, offering a wealth of resources, information and training. The Gateway aims to shine a light on challenges that teachers and SENCOs face, helping them to focus on individual needs rather than a fixation with labels.

The Gateway also offers SENCOs more in-depth information on the new Code of Practice and updating SEN policy, building on the starting points for debate provided in this book. The initiative is supported by organisations such as:

- Dyslexia SpLD Trust
- Dyspraxia Foundation
- National Autistic Society
- Achievement for All (3As)
- Anti-Bullying Alliance
- NATSIP (National Sensory Impairment Partnership)
- DfE.

Given that the National Award for SENCOs remains a mandatory requirement, the Gateway offers all SENCOs, but especially those new to the role, a lifeline of support.

For class teachers, the Gateway also offers materials as publishers place details of their products on the site, introducing schools to the most up-to-date SEND learning resources.

Chapter summary

Whilst SEND early identification remains a guiding principle, every child needs opportunities to learn without intervention first, through QFT. Few young children who initially reverse letters turn out to be dyslexic, and not all children who prefer their own company are autistic. An effective learning environment recognises rights for children to be themselves within a flexibly managed system for all.

Quality first teaching is now seen as the priority area for SEND development, but creating a SEND-friendly classroom that addresses the needs of all — with and without SEND — is an awesome task. Teachers often feel they need thirty pairs of hands! When schools work together to share inclusive QFT solutions, parents and educationalists can be reassured that SEND diagnosis is given only to those who need it. For SENCOs, helping teachers to create SEND-friendly classrooms is a starting point for meeting all needs.

Part III

Evaluating progress for learners with SEND

Chapter 11

Good progress or underachievement?

How do schools recognise good progress or underachievement for learners with SEND, and what are the key principles for assessing, reporting and evaluating success?

National expectations: Realistic for all?

Amongst the current uncertainty (loss of national curriculum, NC, levels), where are schools now in evaluating SEND attainment? 'Breaking the Link between Special Educational Needs and Low Attainment' stated: 'The majority of children with SEN are working within the (now old) National Curriculum where two levels of progress within a Key Stage is a realistic and achievable goal' (DCSF 2010c, p. 21). As all learners did not achieve that level, how realistic was it? The document conceded that pupils with PMLD and some with SLD, 'will find it more difficult or even impossible' to gain the 'same attainment levels as their peers' (p. 20).

With reference to Table 1.3 (Level 4 achievement), did the 2% of pupils with SLD and 1% with PMLD really achieve Level 4 *independently*? I doubt it, but if so, did their SEND assessments accurately reflect their potential? Furthermore, did anyone think to question the unlikely accuracy of these particular results? Data that falls outside national norms alerts schools to the difficulties of predicting individual expectations.

What should schools do now that attainment levels have been abandoned as a nationally recognised measure?

Assessment from 2015

Following the new National Curriculum, previous assessment levels are no longer 'standard'. It seems likely that end of Key Stage expectations will become the national measure, and that schools will be free to devise their own systems for assessment and evaluation between these. 'National Curriculum and Assessment: Information for Schools' (DfE 2014c) visualises a system that enables schools to:

- Check what pupils have learned;
- Analyse whether learners are on track to meet Key Stage expectations;
- Report regularly to parents.

The Association for Achievement and Improvement through Assessment suggests all assessment should refer back to the content of the curriculum (AAIA 2015).

What is the purpose of assessment? Without purpose, assessment is impossible. AAIA (2015) suggests it should:

- Be integral to teaching and learning;
- Recognise learning as a journey;
- Underpin the potential of all learners to achieve (at whatever level);

- Show clear standards that represent achievement;
- Actively involve learners;
- Focus on learning through regular conversation/interaction;
- Reach beyond knowledge and understanding, to encompass skills, capabilities and attitudes to learning;
- Be constructive and task-related, based on what pupils can do (independently!);
- Generate feedback to learners;
- Result in data/information that is consistent, meaningful and useful for parents and governors.

These principles offer schools a starting point from which to build their own systems.

What will OFSTED expect to see from schools' assessment, recording and tracking? AAIA (2015) suggests that inspectors will not expect any *particular* assessment systems in place as schools are consolidating their personal approaches (p. 191). Inspectors will spend more time looking at pupils' work and talking to staff and school leaders about how they use assessment.

The AAIA reports that inspectors will evaluate how well all pupils are doing against the new Key Stage expectations (AAIA 2015). Schools will need:

- A robust, fully-agreed assessment policy that involves parents, and includes specialised arrangements for learners with SEND;
- Aspirational progress objectives, as well as Key Stage goals;
- A clear sense of direction: how short-term targets meet medium-term outcomes and progress towards long-term aspirations.

How useful are performance descriptors? Are they, in effect, levels by another name? The Government published draft performance descriptors for statutory teacher assessment, on the basis that schools should set high standards for what (all) pupils should achieve at the end of Key Stages (DfE 2014d). Table 11.1 summarises some of the performance indicators as examples. It is thought that P scale and EYFS levels would merge into the first set.

Could descriptors comprise a more accurate picture of skills, knowledge and understanding for SEND learners? Only where performance is independent. The progression descriptors from 'below to mastery' suggest that the Government is now recognising the need for all children, especially those with SEND, to 'master' learning before being moved on. The idea of *mastery* for learners with SEND has never been fully compatible with a curriculum based on levels, towards which all children have been required to move as quickly as possible. Mastery as a vital principle has been sadly neglected. The new assessment system will hopefully seek to embed this key principle for all learners.

'National Curriculum and Assessment' describes the anticipated future of assessment as a move away from the previous absolute measure of two levels of progress (DfE 2014c). The new arrangements are to comprise a relative measure against an average of one hundred. The document lists numerous sources of support for schools working on their new assessment systems.

Table 11.1 Speculating on national performance indicators: KS1

Pupils would demonstrate sufficient evidence of the following:

P scales: Pupils count, order, add, subtract numbers practically; small steps, 3, 5, to 10
EYFS/Reception: Pupils count, add and subtract practically up to 10
Below national standard: Pupils count, order, add, subtract numbers to 20
Towards national standard: Pupils count, order, add, subtract numbers to 100
At national standard: Numbers to 100 understood in greater depth, more facts known
Mastery of national standard: still to 100 but wider range, greater application of numbers at this level
For example, adding several, as opposed to only two 2-digit numbers. Also adding 3-digit numbers

Formative and summative assessment

Assessment includes both formative and summative data. Formative accumulates day-to-day feeding into summative assessment at the end of each term, year or Key Stage.

Formative assessment enables schools to track progress, evaluate standards of teaching and learning and report accurately to parents and OFSTED. Without efficient and effective formative assessment, there can be no summative results that stem purely from ongoing teaching and learning, as standardised tests are completely isolated from what children can do. For all children, closely observed formative assessment is the key to unlock achievement.

What might be included in formative data collection? 'Assessment for Learning' (DCSF 2008b) identified three underpinning elements that will always feature:

Day-to-day

- Ongoing responses to learning lesson by lesson;
- Objectives for each lesson made explicit and achievement noted;
- Use of peer and self-assessment;
- Learners engaged and given immediate feedback;
- Range of evidence gathering; for example, notes from observations, samples of work, photos, discussions between staff and parents.

Periodic: termly, or half-termly

- Evidence from personal plan reviews;
- Tracking against national performance descriptors;
- Adjusting medium-term planning.

Transitional (annually or across Key Stages)

- Evidence from annual reviews (EHCPs);
- Reporting to follow-on teachers and parents/carers;
- Matching performance data to summative evidence; for example, standardised tests.

How do schools assemble data that leads to summative assessment? It means that schools have to place assessment at the heart of most lessons and record evidence as it happens. Formative assessment is written in the present tense, not the past. Does this lead to a fresh way of thinking for teachers and pupils, as teaching/learning and assessment merge? Or could schools end up with assessment overkill that takes much of the heart and freshness out of teaching/learning, if just about everything is evaluated?

Formative assessment (Assessment for Learning; AfL), is what happens in classrooms, at the seat of learning. AfL differs from summative assessment, not least, in that the latter is far removed from learning activities.

How can standardised tests be used to complement AfL? Tests have the potential to:

- Predict future performance;
- Justify low attainment;
- Confirm the validity of formative data, rubber-stamp other evidence;
- Conflict with formative data to alert schools that something is not right;
- Compare achievement against norms: potential (intelligence) against actual learning;
- Identify/confirm a special educational need when used by specialists for this purpose;
- Offer schools a blanket picture of collective performance: for year groups, vulnerable groups and Key Stage cohorts.

Standardised tests must be interpreted with care. How useful are reading/spelling ages for an individual, except to compare that child with others? What does a fall in reading age from 7.3 to 7.1 for example, tell teachers about reading competency? Slight falls or rises in reading age scores count for very little, unless a downward or upward trend becomes significant over time. A pupil with SLCN, whose standard score for receptive language (using the British Picture Vocabulary Scale) moves from 78 to 84, may suggest progress, but as vocabulary acquisition (words known) differs between children, such a difference is minimal.

Standardised tests often measure non-verbal ability: intelligence. Might a lower than average non-verbal score lower teachers' expectations? Where such tests confirm or conflict class-based evidence, what does it suggest? On the other hand, tests that measure potential can be used to *justify* why some learners are not achieving age-related levels, or *question* why achievement is not matching potential. So whilst test results must be interpreted with caution, they do work alongside formative assessment.

Judging expectations for learners with SEND

For which learners with SEND are lower than age-related expectations justifiable? 'Progression Guidance' (DCSF 2009f) stated that analysing SEND progress involves in-depth knowledge, from:

- High expectations
- Accurate assessment
- Age and prior attainment.

The document also called for 'realistic but stretching targets' (p. 41). How do schools judge the degree of 'stretch'? If outcomes and targets are set too high, pupils fail to reach them and teachers are held to account. If too low, they cannot do justice to potential.

So where do schools look for high expectations? How 'high' is realistic? The document suggested prior Key Stage attainment as the starting point (DCSF 2009f). But how accurate is prior attainment? Many factors intervene to throw learners off-track. Yet, unless schools revert to measuring learning potential, schools can only trust in prior attainment. Determining the right degree of 'stretch', using prior attainment, needs accurate data from:

- Quality first teaching observations
- Wave 2/3 interventions
- Achievement of targets from termly/annual reviews.

If QFT tasks and termly targets have been 'realistic but stretching', records will clearly show achievement, and inform longer-term expectations. Too many short-term targets on IEPs have either not been met, or only partly met, suggesting either too little focus, or too much stretch. Too much stretch tends to backfire when learning motivation turns to frustration.

'Progression Guidance' also referred to accurate assessment as the guiding principle (DCSF 2009f), and questions whether 'falling behind' national expectations necessarily equates with SEN. When a child falls behind, should schools first question innate potential or the learning environment? The first search for answers is surely QFT.

The focus on previous national curriculum levels and 'teaching to tests' has not always reflected realistic applications of literacy and numeracy. If prior attainment has been overinflated, follow-on teachers struggle to demonstrate value-added progression. If underrepresented, expectations are likely to be deflated. So prior attainment must be reliable.

How do schools judge whether prior attainment accurately reflects what a child with SEND (or any child) can do? Non-verbal or reading and maths tests have been used for years to check the accuracy of prior attainment, and still have their place within a balanced range of formative and summative assessment tools.

Recognising underachievement

Evidence continues to indicate underachievement amongst SEND and other vulnerable groups. But where there are shortfalls, which children can genuinely achieve better?

Underachievement is commonly defined as a discrepancy between achievement and perceived ability. As a general aim, *no* underachievement is acceptable. Hence, the genuine potential of all children is an essential first base from which to set high, yet realistic, expectations. The difference between SEND and non-SEND underachievers is important because interventions used to address mismatch are radically different.

Could more effective QFT stem the tide of children labelled as SEN? The Code of Practice does provide schools with a system for differentiating between non-SEND underperformers and those who *may* have SEND.

Who are the likely underachievers? 'Addressing Underachievement' identified various groups whose gifts and talents are often not identified or nurtured (DCSF 2009g). They include:

- Children from low socio-economic groups; disadvantaged
- Black and minority ethnic
- Those with English as an additional language
- Those in small schools with limited resources
- Learners with SEN
- Children with medical conditions or disabilities
- Pupils from service families who move schools frequently
- New arrivals
- Pupils who are frequently absent
- Home carers
- Looked-after children
- Children from families undergoing stress
- Children at risk of disaffection and exclusion
- Children with summer birthdays.

Many categories overlap and children with SEND are highly likely to be in other groups. The list reminds us that well-being is a priority when judging supposed underachievement. How much stems from learning difficulties and how much could be eradicated if more attention is paid to well-being and social factors?

So where are we now? For years, society has accepted the above factors as excuses for poor performance. The need now is for schools, alongside educational partners (external specialists, health, social services) to tease out factors that cloud judgement, recognise genuine ability and ensure that every child achieves according to perceived potential, using the pupil premium appropriately.

Having teased out social and well-being factors, which learners with SEND could achieve better if schools set higher expectations? Table 11.2 speculates on this, bearing in mind that SEND learners are far from a homogenous group.

Table 11.2 What might higher expectations help to achieve?

PMLD: Profound and multiple learning difficulties are cognitive. Many PMLD learners progress slowly through the P scales throughout their schooling, but could some progress faster?

SLD: Significant cognitive impairment often affects language, as well as other generalised skills, and may prevent most SLD learners from achieving average expectations. Most SLD learners should be able to progress through the new National Curriculum for Key Stage 1, but are likely to fall further behind gradually, as the demands become greater.

MLD: These children comprise a larger group. Depending on their levels of cognitive impairment, most of these learners should achieve age-related expectations with appropriate support.

Table 11.2 continued

SpLD, dyslexia: Cognitive limitations may limit achievement in specifically affected areas, where moderate or severe. Mild dyslexia should not impede development at all. Pupils with dyslexia should achieve well in areas of learning that are not affected.

Autism: With social and communication barriers removed, there is no reason why learners with at least average cognitive ability should not achieve well. There are no excuses for low achievement for the majority of pupils with ASD.

DCD: With DCD barriers removed, learners with dyspraxia should achieve national expectations.

SLCN: Speech, language and communication present the biggest barriers to learning. Yet, provided the SLCN needs are addressed, unless a child has a specific disorder, as opposed to a delay, most pupils with SLCN could perform much better.

HI and VI: Where sensory impairment is the only area of difficulty, most HI and VI learners should achieve at least average expectations.

PD: Where physical difficulties are not accompanied by other types of learning difficulty, and if PD learners receive access to all learning opportunities, their physical difficulties need not impact on achievement at all.

SEMH: When the learning difficulties that often cause challenging behaviours are addressed, most SEMH learners should achieve their potential. SEMH alone is no reason to accept below-average attainment.

I have come to believe that significant cognitive learning difficulties are the only justifiable reason for less than average attainment. Most other learning barriers can and must be swept away.

Eradicating underachievement for SEND learners

I believe there are five main strands, for SENCOs to take a leading role. They are:

- Remove individual barriers as far as possible;
- Sever the link between SEND and low expectations; aim high!
- Promote seamless interaction amongst Waves 1, 2 and 3;
- Ensure a balance of formative and summative assessment alongside the SEN Code of Practice graduated response;
- Link assessment with provision-mapping.

Some important questions:

- How do we know when pupils have improved? Where does evidence come from?
- Does the improvement represent good progress for each learner?
- What is each SEND learner's absolute best?
- How does the SEND system link with whole-school assessment?
- How does assessment fit with wave interventions?

SEND data needs to be built up — from short, to medium, to longer term — using Wave 1 formative sources:

- Achievement in language, literacy and mathematics;
- Achievement across other curricular subjects;
- Progress in areas that form barriers: language, self-help, social and communication skills, listening and attention.

Evidence may conflict. One teacher may have observed skills and knowledge that another does not. Children with SEND do not demonstrate achievements in the same way across different subjects, so writing samples need to show range. Reading data also needs to come from different text types. Range and variety are important.

Who collects the range of evidence from QFT?

- Teachers and TAs?;
- Pupils: feedback from teaching, personal evaluations;
- Parents/carers, from homework observations and behaviours at home.

Not all information forms useful evidence. The bulk needs to be boiled down to what is significant. Either too much, or irrelevant data can deflect attention away from the assessment focus. The efficiency of the QFT data collection relies on all staff knowing what is contextually significant, and recording and reporting within given timescales.

Data also needs to be collected from Waves 2 and 3. How is this mass of data to be collected, recorded and submitted in usable form for reviews? Where is the data stored and who has access?

Progress on SEND achievement may be evaluated differently by those who stand to gain, or lose. Stakeholders include:

- Class teachers: pupil progress reflects on their QFT;
- Teaching Assistants: intervention outcomes;
- Managers (including SENCOs), who may be judged on their support of the three waves;
- Heads/Senior staff, who require whole-school results;
- Learners, whose achievement influences their life chances;
- Parents, who desire the best progress for their children.

To satisfy all stakeholders, the collecting of achievement data needs to be accurate and transparent. AfL data needs to:

- Identify either good progress or underachievement of SEND learners;
- Alert class teachers and SENCOs to shortfalls immediately;
- Enable progress of vulnerable groups to be tracked and monitored regularly;
- Inform senior leaders how well the whole school is doing.

Adequate or good progress?

How does good progress differ from adequate? How is evaluation for *individual* SEND learners measured differently from that of non-SEND learners? Should good progress:

- Represent narrowing of the age-related achievement gap: SEND and non-SEND?
- Control the gap and prevent it growing wider year-on-year?
- Be similar to others with the same difficulties, if below the majority of non-SEND?
- Match or better the pupil's own previous rate of progress?
- Ensure greater access to the curriculum?
- Demonstrate improvement in personal, self-help and social skills?
- Demonstrate improvements in behaviour?
- Show a greater likelihood of leading to accreditation and/or employment?

What do these questions depend on? Table 11.2 represents my views on which types of learners could do better. Cognitive difficulties offer more justification for below-average achievement than non-cognitive. Can children with PMLD or SLD really narrow the achievement gap between themselves and their non-SEND peers? If so, is that rate of progress evaluated under the same conditions, from solely independent achievement? Otherwise, can it count as progress? For SEND learners with difficulties other than cognitive, I believe that once barriers are removed, most should be either preventing the gap from growing wider, or gradually narrowing it.

The above list implies that progress for SEND learners needs to represent broader improvements. 'Your Child, Your Schools, Our Future' also suggested that measuring progress is not confined to academic learning (DCSF 2009d). It includes:

- Improved attendance
- Improved behaviour
- Reductions in bullying
- Development of friendships
- Increased participation in extra-curricular activities.

All of the above impact hugely on academic achievement. Measuring progress through wider outcomes invites schools to take a broader look at SEND success.

How do specialist summative assessments help schools to make evaluative judgements of 'adequate' or 'good'? Table 11.3 contains the kind of evidence that might be provided by specialists from SEN support services, to supplement schools' formative data.

Table 11.3 Example of external specialist assessment: Child aged 6.9

Receptive vocabulary: standard score 97; within the average range
Phonological awareness: standard score 90; within the average range
Auditory memory: standard score 74; very low
Non-verbal ability: standard score 72 is very low, but this score should be treated with caution at such a young age
Information processing speed: standard score 69; suggests that this child may have problems with processing information

Some scores in Table 11.3 are way below average. A non-verbal standard score of 72 (average 100) suggests that a child does not have average potential. Scores for auditory memory and information processing are also low. Scores such as these have done much to reduce learner expectations over many years, generating complacency, or, when children are performing badly, being used as justifiable reasons why. The principle of high expectations invites all schools to keep a fully open mind. Such a young child could emerge with a vastly improved set of standardised scores by the end of Key Stage 2, having strived successfully towards high expectations, with excellent QFT, effectively implemented interventions and accurate formative tracking.

Measuring progress in the smallest steps

Small-step assessment still uses the P Scales (originally DfEE 2001, but now DfE 2014i) to measure progress below Level 1 of the National Curriculum. These targets continue to measure progress for children who are not ready to access Year 1 learning. The P Scales were originally designed as summative assessment using a 'best fit' approach and have been brought up to date to reflect the new assessment arrangements.

Performance Indicators for Valued-Added Target Setting (PIVATS) (Lancashire County Council 2015) is a small-step assessment tool that has stood the test of time. This tool further splits each P level into five sublevels. PIVATS now reflects the new National Curriculum, with changes from the old Level 1 upwards. It includes a moderation folder, available as a hard copy or on CD Rom, with commentary and support evidence.

Other small-step measurement tools include:

- Small Steps Summative Assessment (B Squared 2015b);
- Early Steps Summative Assessment, from birth to the EYFS (B Squared 2015c);
- Connecting Steps: Sample Assessment Pages, Core Subjects: English, Maths and Science (B Squared 2015a) also splits each P level into a number of smaller step assessment objectives.

These resources enable learners at the very lowest levels of achievement (PMLD and some SLD) to be included within whole-school evaluation. Whilst small-step assessment tools offer summative measures of performance, they also remind us that QFT may sometimes rely on teaching/learning objectives being tracked back to their simplest beginnings, as illustrated in Table 11.4 on writing.

Table 11.4 Tracking writing back to the simplest levels

Marks on paper show understanding of the difference between pictures and writing
Marks on paper are accompanied by the child telling an adult what they mean
Marks include a greater range of shapes: straight, angled, curved
Some marks start to represent letters
A greater proportion of letter-like shapes
Clear letters are placed randomly amongst the letter-like shapes
Some letters are placed strategically amongst others; for example, letter 'f' for fish
Spaces start to appear between the attempted words
Writing shows clusters of letters placed clearly and consistently to represent words
Attempted words shows more strategic placing of letters to represent sounds; for example, at the ends of words, as well as at the beginning
Words start to be grouped together regularly in a meaningful way
Writing starts to include a range of phrases
Phrases start to be linked into simple sentences
Letter formation and national curriculum writing develops

These tools also offer valuable training for teachers in tiny-step progression, and enable schools to report accurately on learners for whom the achievement gap will inevitably widen with age.

Matching evaluation to Code of Practice provision

How does both formative (AfL) and summative evaluation help SENCOs to manage the Code's graduated response? There needs to be a strategic accumulation of evidence that feeds into each stage, as illustrated in Table 11.5. At each stage, SENCOs and teachers need to ask:

- Is this child achieving the best they can, or does data indicate underachievement?
- Is the evidence reliable?
- Has the provision-mapping been the best?
- Have all staff contributed effectively and efficiently to the provision?
- Are we satisfied that the child cannot improve on the results?

When the search for underachievement is ongoing and widely spread, schools are more likely to find it.

Table 11.5 Accumulating evidence for Code of Practice responses

Collecting evidence	Judging achievement
Day-by-day: • significant data-gathering from all staff and parents • QFT changes made where necessary	From prior knowledge of what child can do: • ongoing judgements of progress? • on track with day-to-day learning? • records from all staff, parents, pupils?
Termly reviews: • formative data from QFT and Wave 2/3 interventions collated into evidence for parents and pupils • may be supported by summative evidence	From collation of term's evidence: • Do targets achieved indicate that prior knowledge was within range or not? • Have expectations been too high or too low? • Does any summative evidence support or conflict with formative data? • Does provision map need amending? • Does child stay at this stage, or move to different level of support?
Annual reviews for children with EHCPs: • evidence from termly reviews feeds into annual outcomes • accompanied by more formative data from QFT, Wave 2/3 interventions • supported by summative evidence from external specialists	From previous review and new evidence: • Does learning show how termly targets have led to annual outcomes? • Have outcomes been achieved or not? • What does additional formative data indicate? • Does summative evidence support or conflict with previous reviews and updated formative data? • Has best possible progress been made? • Does EHCP provision need amending?
Yearly evaluation for children on SEN support: • evidence from termly reviews • formative data from QFT • summative evidence • evidence from interventions	From previous review and new evidence: • Does termly learning show smooth progression to end-of-year achievement? • Is child on track to meet end of Key Stage expectations or not? • How can child be placed back on track? • Has best possible progress been made? • Does any summative evidence support or conflict with formative data? • Does provision map need amending?
End of Key Stage: • More updated formative evidence • Previous annual evidence	From annual and new formative evidence: • Has child achieved age-related KS descriptors? • If not, has progress been the best possible? • Does the child's achievement represent a realistic summative appraisal of progress? • What needs to be done in the next Key Stage?

From individual to whole-school progress

Any underachievement of SEND or otherwise vulnerable pupils impacts upon the whole school. Lamb recommended that schools should not obtain a good or outstanding judgement from OFSTED, where outcomes for learners with SEND are not good enough (DCSF 2009e). Evidence sought may include:

- Staff training: how has this impacted on pupil achievement?
- How curriculum changes have enabled improved access for SEND learners;
- How personalisation strategies have improved outcomes;
- How high expectations have led to improved outcomes;
- How SEN funding, with that for vulnerable groups, has supported achievement;
- Parent/carers' and pupils' views.

Schools need rock-solid evidence to show why some learners have not, and maybe cannot, achieve average expectations, and that such learners have, nevertheless, achieved the best they can.

OFSTED looks for evidence that all aspects of SEND policy and practice have been evaluated for *impact*; for example:

- How have improvements in QFT impacted on achievement?
- What has been the impact of class TAs?
- How have additional interventions impacted on progress?
- How have attendance and behaviour impacted on progress?

Given that evaluating outcomes for individuals with SEND and other vulnerable groups represents the end of the provision-mapping cycle, evaluation should track back to the beginning: the next audit. The cycle of assess–plan–do–review needs to start all over again.

Resources for assessment and reporting

How do schools manage the entire system in larger schools? Luckily SENCOs have had resources to hand for years.

RAISEonline (Reporting and Analysis for Improvement through School Self-Evaluation: www.raiseonline.org) has been used by SENCOs as a tool to judge how well they are doing, and to set expectations for individuals and identified groups. It has also been used by:

- Inspectors, to help them understand the school before they visit;
- Local Authorities, to judge school performance;
- School Improvement Partners (SIPs), to understand the schools they work with.

RAISEonline allows schools to judge their own performance against national performance, from a report that provides contextual data, progress and attainment measures, and 'forward-looking' estimates for school users to interrogate. A further strength is the facility to look at how particular types of interventions have impacted on performance.

This fully updated resource is a secure evaluation system that can be matched with provision-mapping to make the whole process as simple as possible.

School Pupil Tracker Online (SPTO; www.spto.co.uk) also claims to be a whole-assessment solution and is used by many primary schools. This resource claims to do what all SENCOs need a 'workmate' to do. It:

- Keeps information in one secure place
- Ties together the whole assessment and evaluation journey
- Allows data to be extracted easily
- Is easy to use
- Is quick to personalise for individuals.

Chapter summary

This chapter has attempted to help SENCOs and colleagues judge the difference between good progress and underachievement for all learners. What is the school's agreed concept of 'underachievement'?

- Are learners judged against their own potential or against national expectations?
- Is a pupil who continues to progress below average, but according to personal potential, underachieving?
- Are all pupils who perform below-average underachieving?

In my view, 'underachievement' should describe children who are not achieving what they are genuinely capable of, regardless of how far removed from national standards that achievement is.

As schools get to grips with new national standards, it may be helpful to consider why levels have been rightfully abandoned. Oates (2014) offers these reasons:

- Other high-achieving nations study fewer things in greater depth. The new National Curriculum is therefore more rigorous, emphasising deeper learning around central concepts and ideas;
- Original assessment has been overinfluenced by labelling pupils ('level 2' or 'level 3');
- Too much focus on moving through the attainment levels at a fast pace, without ensuring that all children were ready to move to the next stage;
- The validity of a system that is averaged out (into levels) is low.

Oates further states that teachers need to become experts in assessing learning and probing pupils' understanding, whilst pupils needs to produce more 'stuff' that can be evaluated.

We should welcome this new emphasis on deeper learning. Pupils should be encouraged to make connections between ideas, explore beneath the surface and interrogate to find meanings. The rush to get through the curriculum and achieve levels has not always allowed this type of depth.

I personally hope the new performance descriptors include stages of 'working towards, at or mastery', to ensure for each learner the deeper depth that is particularly important for learners with SEND. Learning must not be rushed.

At the end of the day, measurement itself does not produce good progress nor prevent underachievement. Effective teaching and learning do!

Chapter 12

Developing pupil voice and independence

Why pupil voice? Children and young people are major stakeholders in education. Schools and settings exist solely for them, and the purpose of schools is to secure a potentially bright future for all learners. It is strange that, traditionally, learners have exerted the least influence over how schools have promoted their life chances and aspirations, until now!

Giving all pupils an extended voice

Improved pedagogy and personalisation relies on all pupils gaining the confidence and independence to 'become partners in their own learning, to understand what they are learning and why' (DfES 2007).

Spread liberally throughout the new Code is the requirement to consult and include pupils at each stage of the 'assess, plan, do, review' process. The Code's principles include the requirement for schools to enable learners to participate in decision-making, with support where needed.

Does the new National Curriculum, with its emphasis on deeper understanding of central concepts and ideas, imply a new dimension, an opportunity for learners to reconsider their role in the educational process? I think it does! School stakeholders (and OFSTED) have the same aim: for all learners to succeed. Pupil voice represents a moral and practical imperative for schools to loosen up.

How far does pupil voice include entitlements and responsibilities? Should entitlements start from an educational system that:

- Treats all learners with respect?
- Enables them to enjoy learning and achieve their best?
- Places well-being at the heart of learning?
- Promotes a sense of belonging within the school community?
- Equips all learners for adult life?

This would imply that all learners:

- Take part in decisions that shape their future;
- Have their views taken into account and are supported to express them.

Alongside entitlements should responsibilities include:

- Respect for other cultures, beliefs, views, however different?
- Respect for the diverse needs of everyone?
- Taking a greater part in community activities?
- Helping to shape school policy and practice?
- Accepting personal responsibility for their progress?

Where staff agree, how might it happen? Pupils could debate issues that influence their own learning environment; for example:

- Disability: who may be disabled and how to support them;
- SEN: how we learn differently and why some learners need extra support to succeed;
- Issues to do with equality.

What about community? Could this develop by pupils:

- Taking part in local community activities?
- Visiting businesses and interviewing people about their jobs?
- Helping to resolve community-based problems alongside local people?

So much of school learning is isolated from the community in which it will be applied. Citizenship needs regular practice so that learners experience a smooth flow between school and adult life. Formal 'work experience' is not enough.

Learners helping to shape school policy and practice might include:

- Developing a culture of togetherness: staff and pupils striving towards the same outcomes;
- Extended participation in areas that help them to become better learners: citizenship, personal, social, health and economic lessons, social/emotional development;
- Debating policy: health and safety, inclusion, SEND, discipline, school uniform;
- Pupils helping to solve *real* problems around school: bullying, litter;
- Taking part in the provision-mapping process where possible.

Taking personal responsibility involves pupils in:

- Knowing what they need to learn and why;
- Knowing how they, and others, learn best, and understanding differences;
- Knowing when and how to ask for help;
- Knowing how to adjust learning to suit different contexts and social situations;
- Using ICT and other tools to research (today's learners need to find information).

What might be the outcomes? One outcome from extended pupil voice is to learn that individual views are not always shared, and collective decision-making often means going with the majority. Pupils will appreciate taking part if their opinions are treated with respect and they are given feedback, with reasons for decisions and anticipated improvements.

If pupils were to debate some of the above issues, would respect, social and communication skills, and improved achievement for all result? The probability is very high, although schools would need to loosen the mould of practices designed to secure control.

Extending pupil voice heightens potential for all academic learning, not to mention the social and communication skills that develop alongside. Pupil power is not entirely risk-free. Yet, without risk there is no change, and no significant narrowing of the achievement gap.

Developing pupil voice for learners with SEND

Some pupils with SEND or in vulnerable groups need support to shape outcomes. Any new role requires training. How can pupils' voices be heard at whole-school level? Some pupils may not have the confidence to seek a 'shouting' role, but all learners can be heard at 'whispering' level. Children with SEND are often underrepresented in activities such as:

- Before and after-school clubs; helping to organise activities;
- Membership of the school council;
- Membership of working groups that shape policies.

All SEND learners can be helped to contribute to decisions that affect personal well-being and achievement, and school results will be the better for it.

Having set up safe, well-managed situations, how could pupils with SEND learn to maximise their opportunities? Some may need:

- Help with language and protocols of debate;
- Coaching in focused listening and appropriate response;
- Support to take notes and weigh up key points;
- Support to access the information that enables them to make decisions;
- Help with questionnaires and other opinion-giving tools.

What would extended pupil voice look like? Would observers note:

- More children talking to adults about strengths and weaknesses?
- More children able to give and receive feedback, and act on it independently?
- More confident learners, better able to learn from their mistakes?

No longer are pupils mere 'receivers' of information. The new National Curriculum requires deeper, more extended thought processes: reasoning, analysis, hypothesis, projection, speculation, evaluation. While some learners with cognitive difficulties may not be capable of extended reasoning, they can learn to be active.

Learners could have a more prominent voice in:

- How to complete tasks and what to do when finished;
- Keeping the classroom tidy and organised;
- Where to sit for different lessons: might there be choices?
- How to work as a member of a group for different purposes or topics;
- Rules of communication: politeness and helping each other;
- How to be a 'buddy' for peers who need help;
- How to learn independently and what to do when help is needed.

Although teachers strive to get QFT right, for them to become experts in assessment as Oates (2015) suggests, learner feedback is vital. Teachers need pupils to:

- Help them adjust their planning where necessary, getting teaching styles and objectives just right;
- Feed back to them about lessons;
- Help each other, using self- and peer assessment.

How should pupil voice influence provision-mapping? To what extent should children have choice, or be able to feed back their views? Consider:

- A school uses the same resource for phonic intervention but a pupil dislikes it so progress is slow;
- A secondary learner has an assigned TA but feels embarrassed and fails to respond;
- A pupil in Year 9 is taken out of French for extra Maths but feels resentful;
- A child with reading difficulties is on a low readability scheme she cannot engage with;
- A Year 6 child is taught in the Year 4 class — hugely affecting self-esteem.

Teachers clearly do know which interventions usually produce the best outcomes, but where pupils are unhappy and alternatives exist, pupil voice as part of the provision-mapping system is an investment.

A study detailing the experiences of disabled learners and their families highlighted what pupils with disabilities wanted from additional support (Lewis *et al.* 2007, p. 5). Young people at a specialised residential college yearned for greater independence, even if it involved risk-taking and uncertainty, often in contrast to their parents. Pupils in school often valued their support, but felt resentful about asking teachers repeatedly for the same things (as if they had not been complied with). Other young people wanted more flexible deployment of adult helpers.

Transition to a new school can be traumatic, so SEND pupils may need to air their anxieties:

- What happens on the first day?
- How do I get to my new school?
- How do I find my way around the building, and what happens if I get lost?
- What are the lunch arrangements?
- Who will help me if I have a problem?
- Who do I talk to about bullying?
- Where are the toilets?
- How will I cope with different teachers?
- How will I make new friends?

These can be perplexing issues for pupils with autism or social/communication difficulties. Talking about anxieties *before* transition helps such learners to practise their communication skills in a familiar, comfortable setting, prior to the 'newness'.

What proportion of children and young people attend their progress reviews? Of those who do, how effectively do they influence outcomes? Very little, in my experience. To be an effective voice at reviews, learners need to:

- Have been prepared beforehand: when the meeting is, what they have to do, what questions they may be asked;
- Have discussed learning regularly, to feel comfortable talking about their strengths and weaknesses with adults, and be responsive to constructive criticism;
- Recognise the review as a forum for personal development and aspirations;
- Recognise the review as an evaluation of their work over the previous term or year;
- Have formed their own views: personal barriers, targets achieved or not, effectiveness of interventions, what has or has not been successful.

With coaching, I believe most children can start to think about learning in these ways from Key Stage 1, or even earlier. The Code refers to children being able to make choices from an early age so that from Year 9, young people can become 'explicit elements of conversations' between professionals and families (1.39).

Finally, with regard to pupil voice, annual reviews have become more pupil-centred, especially at secondary level. Person-centred reviews place young people at the heart of decision-making. They should be encouraged to organise their own reviews, and with support prepare invitations, collate samples of work, or discuss their aspirations and how best to achieve them. A tool kit (Children's Society 2009) and booklet (Barnardo's/Yorkshire Partnership 2006) offer guidance on involving disabled learners in reviews, with resources for the professionals working with them.

Despite their problems the majority of pupils with SEND can become active learning partners, but the process needs to start early.

Developing pupil independence

Pupil voice and independence are as two sides of the same coin. What does independent working look like to observers? Are more pupils with SEND:

- Working without adults for a greater proportion of time?
- Using a range of strategies when stuck to get themselves 'unstuck'?
- Using tools to support learning: number lines, thesauruses, sentence scaffolds?
- Using checklists to assess their work before adults see it?
- Making informed choices: order of tasks, selecting from a range of strategies?

Independence is a mindset. It's about pupils saying, 'I can do this myself'. What could be the benefits? As children work more independently in class, would that create more time for adults to:

- Observe unaided learning and make more informed assessments?
- Talk to individuals during the course of the lesson?
- Manage behaviour better, as fewer pupils would be waiting for adult attention?
- Spend more time developing the deeper concepts and ideas embedded within the new National Curriculum?
- Help learners with SEND to apply intervention work to QFT?
- Stand back and manage classroom learning in a more relaxed way?

Independence is not something that schools focus on naturally. Yet, the unnecessary dependence of many children on adult support has often limited curricular efficiency and stunted learning. Classrooms could be transformed if all SEND learners are trained to work as independently as they can. The success of the new 'deeper learning' curriculum depends on it. Table 12.1 speculates how independence could apply to pupils with SEND.

Table 12.1 SEND independent behaviours

SLCN: Ask for word meanings. Asks questions from card during class discussions. Uses simple thesaurus to expand vocabulary. Uses assigned 'buddy' support.

Dyslexia: Uses LSCWC spelling strategy. Jots effectively to support poor memory. Uses times tables square. Uses mind-mapping to draft writing ideas. Uses a diary as an organising tool.

ASD: Uses 'time out' cards appropriately. Organises own workstation. Tells adult when needs to work alone or differently. Uses emotion cards to communicate/resolve issues.

Dyspraxia: sets up own laptop for writing. Gets out special scissors and other equipment.

SEMH: Operates 'time out' system with adult. Self-evaluates behaviour. Takes responsibility for classroom tasks.

MLD: Solves a two-step Maths problem using prompt cards. Works for 20 minutes without adult support.

SLD: Works without adult for up to 10 minutes. Completes piece of work without adult support. Recognises a danger and informs adult. Gets out own equipment.

HI/VI: Organises special equipment. Sits where there is least noise interference. Chooses where vision is best without waiting to be told by adults. Self-organises enlarged font.

PD: Places wheelchair in best place in class. Organises own peer support as needed.

Independence at each Key Stage

Most learners develop independence naturally. They:

- Understand their own learning styles and help adults to know them;
- Accept age-appropriate responsibility;
- Engage in discussions about their own strengths and weaknesses;
- Accept mistakes as part of learning;
- Avoid reliance on others;
- Take pride in their progress and strive to succeed.

Pupils with SEND often need help to do these things. However, I have come to believe that most benefit greatly from knowing and coming to terms with their difficulties, in the complete trust and confidence that adults are there to help them develop self-coping strategies that will last for life.

So how can schools and settings start their journey to increase independence for learners with SEND? Firstly, there needs to be a policy to which all staff adhere. Some starting points:

- Establish a whole-school culture of independent learning;
- Train pupils how to evaluate their work using tools: for example, writing checklists;
- Scribe for learners only when absolutely necessary, not to speed up tasks;
- Insist on all learners working without adult support for varying amounts of time;
- Reward independent behaviours: emphasise positive examples and make a fuss;
- Ensure pupils have tools to support their difficulties: number lines, word lists, tables squares, pictures or diagrams that help to 'fix' tasks, memory aids, writing scaffolds;
- Ensure all activities are achievable so that independence can happen;
- Model tasks prior to independent work;
- Ensure task instructions are clear; write them down;
- Have clear expectations for each child.

The aim is *never* to use additional adults to help a child to achieve work at a higher level than they are capable of performing alone. I have come across many Teaching Assistants, who, with the best intentions, have helped children to do 'class-based' work at too high a level, that is then marked by a teacher as the child's own. Where pupils have been unduly supported to complete tasks that are above them, assessment through 'prior learning' becomes meaningless.

From a culture of independence, QFT can be further enhanced through the three inclusion factors: appropriate challenges; removal of access barriers; and the accommodation of diverse learning styles. Some age-appropriate ideas are as follows:

At the Early Years Foundation Stage:

- Making simple choices: Do I need my coat at playtime? Which activity shall I do next?
- Sorting equipment by themselves;
- Engaging in talk that needs decision-making: What kind of story shall we have today?
- Giving opinions on what they find easy or hard, or what they like and dislike.

Making sensible choices is a first important skill.

At Key Stage 1, build on the above, plus:

- Encourage more specific self-responsibility for learning;
- Generate sensitivity in relationships, through group working/communication skills;
- Start to develop skills for discussing/resolving difficulties, to support progress reviews.

At Key Stage 2, as above, plus:

- As subject learning becomes more complex, strengthen pupils' skills of asking for explanation;
- Reinforce the idea of 'inner' learning, guided and controlled by pupils themselves. Teachers can only control 'outer' learning;
- Strengthen pupils' ability to use language effectively: challenge, question, explain, describe, persuade or summarise;
- Refine pupil's skills in talking about their own strengths and weaknesses, as some learners gradually fall further behind, self-esteem becomes more of an issue;
- Help learners with SEND to understand themselves, their types of difficulties, how to cope with them, their learning styles, and teach them self-coping strategies.

Secondary, as above, plus:

- Further develop self-coping strategies: adults need to step back and allow learners with SEND to solve their own problems (with advice and support where necessary);
- Teach pupils how to develop their own personalised learning and how to help others to understand their individual needs;
- Teach learners with SEND how to organise and chair their own reviews, with support;
- Coach learners in how to write their own termly and annual reports (supplemented by those of teachers).

Is this last bullet point a step too far? I don't think so. If children have been encouraged to review their learning cumulatively throughout school, reporting on themselves (as part of English work) should not be a problem. Such tasks offer children a genuine context for written communication: their teachers and parents. What better motivation could students have to demonstrate their best written work?

Schools need to give secondary learners with SEND the reins to become fully independent young people. As they gain in confidence, their efforts can only surprise and delight us. Far too many young adults with SEND are wrapped in cotton wool throughout school, and emerge into the real world without skills to cope.

The sensitive deployment of TAs is also crucial. Dispensing with the traditional 'SEN table' in classrooms encourages independent learning for the following reasons:

- Placing all SEN pupils at one table encourages the perception that all their difficulties are the same;
- Placing a TA at the 'SEN table' encourages learned helplessness;
- At the same table, children tend to engage more with the adult than with other learners;
- The TA is tempted to do more for the child than what is needed;
- It is difficult to assess work accurately from high expectations, as work is likely to be more 'adult-prompted'.

Teaching Assistants remain an indispensable feature of most classrooms, but their presence has too often fostered a culture of dependency amongst SEND learners. Most learners will rise admirably to the independence challenge if given the training, encouragement and freedom to do so.

Table 12.2 shows my model for developing independence in all schools and settings, adapted from Edwards (2001).

Table 12.2 Making independence happen

Prioritise independence: place it at the top of the school development plan, feature it as a staff training day to agree policy and present it to learners as a whole-school initiative to raise achievement.

Expect it and be consistent: set targets for consistent independent behaviour across the school; ensure these transfer into all classrooms and support all pupils to achieve them.

Model it: ensure pupils know which aspects of behaviour subscribe to the independence focus for each lesson.

Observe/evaluate: record independent behaviours alongside other aspects of AfL.

Provide pupil feedback: 'well done for asking what that word means', or 'this group got out their equipment and put it away really well'.

Reward it: build rewards into the independence programme so that pupils soon see independent learning as crucial to all of their educational development.

Research reminds us that learners can often do far more than expected when provided with opportunities. As Lewis *at al.* (2007) stated, 'on many occasions, there was surprise at the extent to which children were able to communicate their views, and the fullness of these views' (p. 20). In its recommendations, their report concluded that, when approached sensitively, alongside high expectations and aspirations, learners with SEND can become equal players in school policy, practice and evaluation.

Finally, the new Code places independence at the top of the agenda when it comes to preparing young people with SEND for adulthood (DfE/DH 2015). Section 8.1 refers to the young person being able, through reviews, to fully discuss their aspirations, interests and needs, with regard to health, participation in society, making friends, and independent living arrangements: the 'great majority of children and young people with SEN and disabilities, with the right support, can find work, be supported to live independently and participate in their community' (DfE/DH 2015, p. 124). Schools and parents need to encourage these ambitions from the start.

Chapter summary

I believe strongly that learning independence, alongside pupil voice, is key to changing the dynamics of school and learner interaction and in so doing, narrowing that achievement gap that eventually leads to gross inequalities in our society. Yes, the Government clearly does have a vested financial interest in enabling as many young adults as possible to leave schools and colleges able to find work and live in semi-independent housing. But such an aim also represents a much improved quality of life for the young people with SEND, who can achieve such aspirations … and all but the tiniest minority can!

So, if schools have high expectations for all other aspects of learning, then setting similarly high expectations for pupil voice and independence must help to ensure success for all.

Chapter 13

Parents as equal partners

Parental rights, roles and responsibilities in education have been strengthened considerably. Parents are now expected and entitled to exert huge influence on SEND policy and practice as equal partners. What is meant by 'equal partners' and how can schools achieve such equality with all parents, including those who may be hard to reach? Developing equal partnerships with parents and carers has, more than ever before, now become a significant and major part of the SENCO role.

What has been achieved so far?

The Lamb Inquiry (DCSF 2009e) first expressed concerns about the lack of parental satisfaction and confidence in the SEND system and recommended:

- More skilled teachers and better resources for children with SEND;
- A stronger voice for parents: with more and better communication and access to information; parents to be equal partners;
- Greater focus on children's needs;
- A more accountable system: pupil voice strengthened and greater focus on SEND outcomes;
- OFSTED to judge schools as 'good' or better only if outcomes for SEND are also good.

These recommendations have been accepted. The Inquiry outlined many parents' struggles to obtain an education that best fits the needs of their child, and emphasised the value parents placed on staff with expertise to enable their child to achieve, summarised by their overwhelming wish for 'someone who understands my child's needs' (DCSF 2009e, p. 28).

The Lamb Implementation Plan focused on:

- Improving practice within the workforce
- Children's outcomes
- Strengthening engagement with parents
- Strategic local approaches: services working together
- Making the SEND system more accountable.

The Lamb recommendations have already done much to improve practice; for example:

- The focus on high expectations and aspirations, seeking the best achievement for those with the greatest difficulties;
- The IDP continues to improve teaching for pupils who are 'hard to teach';
- The needs of SEND learners are better incorporated into teacher training and induction;
- There have been improvements in pedagogy and personalisation;
- Achievement for All has proved successful and been rolled out nationally;

- The OFSTED 'limiting judgement' places SEND achievement at the top of the agenda;
- Following the Salt Review (2010) greater numbers of teachers are being trained to teach SLD and PMLD learners;
- The role of SENCOs in leading improvements, advising, and training colleagues has been strengthened.

In the wake of all this huge effort by schools and educationalists, there is no easy answer to why the achievement gap is still too wide. Could it be that pupils' and parents' voices need to be more than just 'heard', and central to everything schools do? Are parents now the ultimate solution; the missing link?

Within the spirit of Lamb, how do schools build improved parental confidence? Starting points:

- Honesty: there is a delicate balance between not alarming parents that their child may have SEND and allowing them to think their child is on track if they are not;
- Conversations that are genuinely 'two-way';
- Valuing parents' knowledge about their child and using this to personalise or overcome barriers to learning;
- Tackling problems together: compatibility between school and home is crucial;
- Schools being sensitive to parents' feelings and fears for the future: many parents struggle to accept that their child has a learning difficulty or disability;
- Removal of the parent/professional divide.

The final point has often limited the extent to which parents have been 'equal partners' in education. Many parents feel that their views and opinions are on less of an equal footing than the professionals who, as they may see it, often speak better, know more and have better communication skills (sometimes true). This is because teachers are, in the eyes of parents, 'professionals', who, like doctors, must know best. Parents who think like this are unlikely to try to bridge this professional divide. It is up to schools to reach out to parents who lurk on the sidelines.

Parental involvement in many schools has progressed much further than simply 'informing' or 'liaising with' parents, but it needs to go further still. Parents are the key to unlocking learner potential and schools need to explore the meaning of 'equal partnership'.

Developing parental confidence through the Code of Practice

Liaison with parents has rarely focused on outcomes for learners with SEND. Conversations have often centred around provision, with little emphasis on what that provision was intended to achieve. The legacy of low expectations perhaps? Now that 'high expectations' lead, how should parents be involved in Code procedures?

At the 'initial concern' stage, parents need to know. Many may suspect, from difficulties with homework, or unusual behaviours, that something is wrong and welcome the chance to talk about it. *Without* reference to SEND at this stage, parents, class teachers, and perhaps SENCOs, need to identify together what the problem could be.

Having been involved from this initial stage, parents should have few surprises if their child is later diagnosed with SEND. The essence of 'equal partnership' is to include parents from the beginning and problem-solve together.

How many parents understand the Code of Practice system well enough to be an 'equal' part of it? Very few. I believe parents need help to understand:

- What happens at each stage of the Code's graduated response;
- What class-based intervention is being provided at Wave 1;
- How additional interventions at Waves 2/3 link into Wave 1;

- How their child's personal plan ties into the Code's graduated response;
- What it means when external specialists are brought in;
- What happens at termly and annual reviews;
- What they can do at home.

Too often, parents follow school advice blindly, without questioning it or offering their opinions. Training parents on the Code of Practice is the starting point, as without that basic knowledge, they cannot converse on equal terms.

What about personal plans (IEPs)? I have met numerous parents who have had no idea what the targets mean, not to mention how their child is to be supported to achieve them. Time is a big issue where there are large numbers of children, but if parents do not understand what their child's personal plan is meant to achieve they are, literally, helpless, and schools are missing out on a valuable resource.

A further barrier that gets in the way of parental understanding is jargon. Personal plans need to be written in a pupil and parent-friendly way. Reports by external specialists often challenge the comprehension of the most intelligent parent. What does a standard score of 78 or 114 mean for particular assessments? Even if some parents recognise 100 as average, the implications of scores above or below need explanation.

Do schools sometimes underestimate how well parents can help their child at home? Where parents are given lists of 'tricky' words, they also need to know how to help their child to learn them. What does it actually mean for parents to be told that their child needs to improve comprehension, sentence writing or addition of double-digit numbers? How are parents to do this? As educators, we often assume that parents know when they don't.

Sometimes schools need to tread sensitively. How do we achieve equal partnerships with the parents of children who are:

- Disadvantaged?
- Have emotional difficulties that have their roots in home circumstances?

Communication in such difficult circumstances is not easy. Yet it is parents in difficult circumstances who often need the help of schools the most. Breaking down barriers to create relationships with all parents is fundamental, however long it may take.

Regarding statements, Lamb reported evidence of parents' 'negative and stressful' experiences of statutory assessment (DCSF 2009e, p. 61), as well as statements that were unclear and ambiguous, or not updated enough to reflect a child's changing needs. Michaelson (2015) points out that old reports should not be used to inform EHCPs, as these have not focused sufficiently on *outcomes*. Rewriting statements into EHCPs, with fresh 'outcome-focused' reports, is a valuable opportunity to involve parents from the outset of the EHCP journey.

Lamb also reported that parents need reassurance that staffing arrangements include teachers and assistants with specialist skills and knowledge to support their child's learning needs, and to know the proportion of time spent on their child by the teacher and TA. Parents would also like to see a better focus on outcomes and objectives for wider achievement, rather than purely academic attainment.

While there is no doubt that schools need to build more effective partnerships with parents, achieving it involves a big sea-change in the way that schools approach parental partnership.

Towards an improved parental role

Amongst parents who *do* want to be more involved in their child's achievement are many who do not know how, mainly because they may not understand what their child learns. So what *do* parents need to know? Might schools start by offering workshops on developing basic skills: language, literacy and maths. The following textboxes offer ideas.

Teaching parents how to support maths

For parents of young children, help them to:

- Play with maths!
- Make maths 'real': counting, measuring, weighing around the home and 'out and about'.
- Talk about mathematical language in context: more/less, half/quarter, heavy/light. Half might mean half a packet of sweets, half of a glass of milk or half of a bar of chocolate.
- Bring talk into every activity.
- Consolidate early number concepts: that number 'two' refers to things such as dogs, teddies or sweets, and that numbers are more or less: 5 is more than 4, but less than 7.

Activities:

- Count stairs up to bed.
- Count sweets and biscuits: How many eaten? How many are left?
- Cut cakes into halves or quarters: How many halves? Are they roughly the same size?
- Play games to find different shapes: How many rectangles (windows) can you find? How many circles (clock, plates)?
- Play 'I spy': I spy something that is blue and it's square.
- Play games such as Snap, Dominoes, Happy Families with number and maths concepts.

At Key Stage 1

Help may include the importance of mental computation before using written methods. Learning to use memory is also important.

Activities:

- For memory, place up to 10 objects on a table, child memorises for two minutes, parent takes some away. What is missing?
- Chain game for memory; for example, parent: 'I have 6. What is 2 more?' Child says '8'. Parent: 'Take away 3.' Child should say '5'. Parent: 'double it.' Child says '10'. Each number is derived from the last. Children have to remember the new answer each time.
- Number bonds: games like Snap to match pairs that make 10 (6/4, 8/2).

Emphasise the importance of:

- Language in maths: subtract, take away, minus, difference, less than.
- Practising new ideas until they become secure, as facts: halving and doubling, number bonds, times tables.

Help parents to see 'tens and units' as the first vital step towards understanding higher numerical relationships and solving problems: 10 more than 57; half of 50; the number of tens in 78.

From Key Stage 2 onwards:

Parents can help children to develop a logical sense of the number system: what higher numbers such as 2,398 actually mean as place value; that when adding or multiplying answers must be more, but when dividing, answers must be less. Encourage parents to think through puzzles with their child:

- When we double a number is the answer more or less than what we started with?
- Do squares and rectangles each have four right angles?
- Which is the odd one out? Half of 70, 10×3.5, 2×15 or $100 - 65$?

Odd one out again. Halving a number, adding 20, dividing by 3 or subtracting 10? Answer is 'adding 20' as the others end up with a lesser number. Such questions should encourage logical and thoughtful responses. Help parents to understand the importance of not moving their child on before concepts are secure and mastered, bearing in mind the 'deeper learning' that characterises the new curriculum. Emphasise praise and help parents to show sensitivity to errors while still maintaining motivation. Above all, show parents how to make maths fun and rewarding for their child!

Teaching parents how to support their child's language

Language and learning: Help parents to know that:

- Words help us to think and acquire concepts.
- More immediate concepts help us to understand those that are obscure: if we touch a hot oven, we do not need words to learn not to touch it again. But we cannot form a concept of the moon without more immediate concepts to describe it. A picture is not enough. Without language to describe what we see, hear, touch, taste and smell, as well as what we feel as emotions, and without the words that extend understanding beyond immediate sensory experience (burns from ovens), our knowledge of the world would be severely limited.
- A rich vocabulary is the most precious gift that parents can give to their children.

Language as communication

Help parents to see how language is used in different ways to communicate and how important communication is to all learning. Stress the importance of family talk, from eating to film-going, to resolving issues in productive ways. In our technological world children are becoming better able to communicate with computers and tablets than with people, as talk is being squeezed out of modern society. Parents need to force time to talk between the TV and ICT games. Also, help parents to see how good speaking and listening underpins reading and writing.

Early on, parents need to:

- Talk about everything together: shopping, visiting the doctor or feeding the ducks.
- Speak clearly to help young children recognise different speech sounds.
- Use words as a source of help, comfort and as a source of human interaction.
- Read stories and make reading a warm and cosy experience.

Throughout the foundation stage parents need to help their children use talk to:

- Support learning in a positive way
- Explain feelings and problems
- Develop confidence and independence
- Expand and explore thoughts: What if …? What do we need to bake a cake?
- Talk simply about how things work: the TV needs electricity so we have to plug it in
- Expand and reinforce learning at nursery
- Describe things by colour, size and shape

- Make simple choices and selections
- Give opinions respectfully and develop confidence to make safe, simple decisions
- Solve problems positively.

Throughout Key Stage 1:

- Continue to talk about everything
- Encourage children to talk about school: what they feel good at or need help with, to help maintain self-esteem and motivation
- Expand on new words and concepts, especially in reading, writing and numeracy, reinforcing concepts such as, halve, double, fraction, are important
- Young children often struggle to realise how language and literacy grow together, how sounds/ letters grow into words, phrases and sentences, and how spoken language structures help reading and writing.

Throughout Key Stage 2:

As many more new concepts are introduced across the curriculum, children must recognise when they do not understand and ask an adult for help. Parents can help their children to grow into self-motivated learners with the confidence to use language for different purposes, with different people to:

- Ask questions
- Explain how something works
- Describe objects and events with growing accuracy and range of vocabulary
- Give personal opinions in appropriate ways
- Debate or evaluate something; for example, what is happening around the world

Resolve problems with others in positive ways.

Secondary level:

As subjects become separated, and as reading and writing become a priority, talk must not be squeezed out. Speaking and listening are even more important, in a different way. Parents can help by:

- Continuing to develop high-level vocabulary: more abstract concepts (determination, existence, traditional, civilisation)
- Encouraging young people to listen to the news and discuss national and international events, and evaluate the good and bad of what is happening around them
- Helping young people to use talk to support literacy and other learning
- Making talk available at every opportunity: for praise, comfort, support and reassurance.

Throughout schooling, parents can help to show children that, through effective talk, problems shared really can be problems halved.

Parents will also welcome training in other areas:

- Independence at home
- Responding to homework difficulties
- Managing motivation
- Maintaining their child's self-esteem in the face of significant learning problems.

Parental engagement through culture, policy and practice

Where the culture and ethos of a school make clear that the progress of every individual learner is of equal importance, parental confidence is already part-way there.

Some parents can and want to play a more valued part in policy and school practices that impact on their own child's progress. Lamb recommended that parents should be consulted on policies, so could some parents of learners with SEND become partners in the drafting and review of policies, such as SEND, assessment, inclusion, discipline, well-being, homework or health and safety, as well as the school's policy response to the Equality Act, which must involve parents and learners with disabilities?

More far-reaching and challenging for schools is the possibility of using targeted parental involvement to address specific areas of low achievement. Using the Lamb Inquiry's attainment data (DCSF 2009e, p. 17):

- Below the age of 7, SLCN was the most common area of need, with 42% of children in Key Stage 1 or below receiving external specialist support;
- From age 7 to 11, MLD was the most common, with 34% needing specialist help;
- From age 12 to 17, BESD (now SEMH) was most common, with 34% needing external behavioural intervention.

What do these figures tell us? It seems logical that language/communication features so highly during early learning. We can also see how MLD that may have been masked by language difficulties could have crept up, as teaching demands increased throughout Key Stage 2. It is also easy to see why behavioural difficulties escalate throughout secondary age. These trends continue to exist and schools cannot improve on them without involving parents in more extensive ways. A reduction in SLCN for children under 7 starts in the home. Reducing MLD relies on parents being taught how to back up learning and support cognitive difficulties at home, while a reduction in SEMH depends on absolute home–school consistency with behavioural strategies.

How might this kind of targeted parental support happen? For example, to reduce SLCN in the EYFS and KS1, schools might:

- Invite parents with children in these age groups to an initial meeting to explain the problems, purpose and objectives of the project;
- Train parents how to develop vocabulary and language at each developmental stage;
- Develop with parents, simple 'before and after' evaluation criteria;
- Hold regular meetings with involved parents to discuss progress and offer ongoing support;
- Assign a named person in school to lead the project;
- Make the parental project part of the provision-mapping system.

Variations in confidence would need to be judged sensitively, with some parents starting with smaller-step tasks. Confidentiality would also have to be handled sensitively.

Parent projects could address any area of high-incidence SEN. Clusters of schools working together on parent-based projects, possibly supported by a relevant external specialist, would greatly enhance the value. Just as research has the potential to improve QFT, targeted, home-based support strategies offer fresh and innovative ways for parents to support learning.

How about provision-mapping? By involving parents in strategic ways to support issues highlighted by audits, could outcomes be further enhanced? Parent power may be stronger than we think once it is firmly harnessed and used to target whole-school problems in visionary ways.

Schools could also question the strength and potential of their own or local Parent Teacher Association (PTA). The national PTA goal to 'bring about understanding between parents and schools' constitutes a readily available platform for extending parental involvement, and getting everyone to sing from the same hymn sheet (Parent Teacher Association 2015).

Do schools have SEN parent/carer forums, where parents might get together for mutual support? Many parents of children with SEND feel isolated with the challenges of caring for their loved one. Talking over issues with others in the same boat is helpful.

The Pupil and Parent Guarantees suggested by previous government (DCSF 2009d), while no longer guarantees, should still represent *entitlements*, offering *all* pupils:

- Good discipline, order and safety;
- A broad, balanced and flexible curriculum;
- Teaching that meets their needs;
- Opportunities to take part in cultural and sporting activities;
- An environment where health and well-being are promoted;
- Encouragement and support to express their views.

Such entitlements would offer parents:

- Choice, with proper information and support;
- Home–school agreements outlining *joint* responsibilities;
- Opportunities to fully engage in their children's learning, with information and support;
- Access to a variety of services and facilities, to help them to be *equal* partners.

Parental confidence has the potential to grow naturally from:

- Their trust in the high aspirations that schools place on their learners;
- A culture of equality across the school;
- Well-targeted strategies for communication;
- Opportunities to fully influence school policy and practice.

There has been much research over the years into the effects of parental support on learners' achievements. Harris and Goodall (2007) confirmed that the home environment makes the maximum difference to all pupils' achievements. A further report (DCSF 2008f) suggested that most parents would like to increase their educational involvement, but challenges include barriers such as work commitments (the highest), child-care issues and lack of time.

Schools need to ask themselves:

- How are we communicating to parents that they matter?
- How can we eliminate some of the barriers to parental involvement?

Do parents need to feel they are the *solution*, not the problem?

A report by Sacker (2002) linked the effects on pupil achievement of social class, school and parental involvement with pupils' ages (see Table 13.1), concluding that:

- Parental effect is strongest up to age 7 then declines;
- The school effect increases with pupil age;

- The effect of social class increases slightly with age.

While these results must be treated with caution as they are not new, and we know that the link between schools' parental involvement and social class is complex, they suggest that parental involvement is at its most influential throughout Key Stage 1, and becomes far less influential throughout secondary school, as might be expected. Given that many children with SEND are disadvantaged, and their parental data is likely to be linked with that of social class, we must approach these results with care. However, the overall message is clear: the earlier parents get on board, the more effective their involvement is likely to be as a resource for pupil achievement, and parental engagement makes the greatest difference for learners with SEND.

'The Children's Plan' reminded us that schools do not bring up children; parents do (DCSF 2007). Families therefore need to be at the heart of everything that schools do. Parents are the most powerful improvement lever we have.

Table 13.1 Effect of school, social class and parental involvement on pupil achievement

Age	School effect	Social class	Parental involvment
7	0.05%	0.45%	0.29%
11	0.21%	0.58%	0.27%
16	0.51%	0.61%	0.14%

Finally, Harris (2012) reported interesting data on parental barriers to school involvement and engagement, as illustrated in Table 13.2. This data suggests that the two biggest barriers are lack of school experience, and lack of skills; both easily dealt with by schools. This data should encourage us all to reflect on the best ways to draw parents into the centre of everything schools do.

Table 13.2 Barriers to parental involvement

• School itself 10%	• No education experience 26%	• School not doing enough 1%	• Child attitudes 18%
• Perceived attitude of teacher 17%	• Parents lack of support skills 18%	• Practical issues 3%	• Parents not interested 7%

Chapter summary

This chapter has offered ideas for parents to become more involved with schools on a number of levels:

- Supporting basic skills in general to enhance the effects of QFT;
- Supporting their child's personalised interventions;
- Helping to develop, monitor and evaluate SEND policies and general practices;
- Specific projects to address issues highlighted from the provision-mapping audit.

Most parents should be able and willing to support the first two, with targeted encouragement and training. Armed with the inspiration, confidence and knowledge that schools have given them, they are more likely to enter into the spirit of an enhanced supporting role.

The next two levels demand more. Fewer parents may feel able to get involved at a level that is not directly related to their child's outcomes. Nevertheless, some may welcome with open arms the chance to be at the centre of school action, so schools need to grab hold of these adventurous souls, nourish their needs and train them further.

Parent power is here! The Code of Practice and Equality Act require schools to place parents at the centre of their policy and provision-mapping processes and responses to legislation. Do schools really tap into and make as much use as they could of the huge volume of information parents have about their own child's behaviours, characteristics and personalities, all of which could unlock vital learning potential?

Equal partnership for some schools may mean stepping back and looking at problems more from the parents' perspective and recognising that, sometimes, a parent may know at least as much as the school does. The swift movement towards a policy of genuinely *equal* partnership amongst schools, external specialists and parents needs collaborative strategy, and SENCOs are at the centre.

I hope this chapter has offered useful ideas to stimulate parental policy discussion with all colleagues, and of course, parents.

Conclusion

This book has hopefully generated many issues for discussion, aimed at beating low attainment and narrowing that elusive achievement gap. The following sections summarise key questions from each chapter to support debate.

Chapter 1. Rethinking special educational needs and learning difficulties

The Lamb Inquiry reminds us that 'the education system is living with the legacy of a time when children with SEN were regarded as uneducable. Too often they are set the least demanding challenges' (DCSF 2009e, p. 2). Issues:

- Does our school have high expectations for all, or are we still living with the legacy?
- How does our school identify SEN? Are we too quick to assign SEN labels?
- Do gender, social or ethnic factors unduly influence SEN diagnosis?
- Are strategies in place to identify multifaceted learning difficulties?
- How does our SEN achievement data compare with national norms or similar schools?
- Do all staff have at least a basic understanding of SEN?
- Which of our SEND learners *can* achieve age-related expectations?
- Of those who can't, how do we assess and set expectations that match their potential?

Chapter 2. The new Code: From labels to needs

Beating low attainment depends on the effective management of the Code's graduated response. The future life chances of thousands of children with SEND invite debate on:

- Whether improved identification and provision could further reduce SEND numbers;
- The link between SEN labels and the Code's four broad areas of need: how they interact to support teaching and learning;
- How the COP system could be more effective, bringing policy and practice together;
- How termly/annual reviews could be more effective, with a more active and influential role for parents and learners;
- How our response to the Code is synchronised with provision-mapping and 'waved' intervention;
- How personalised 'additional to and different from' approaches could make that essential difference between success and failure for certain individuals.

Chapter 3. Special educational needs and disability (SEND)

Whose role is it to ensure that the needs of pupils with disabilities are met under the Equality Act? While SENCOs play a substantial role, especially where the Code of Practice and Equality Act overlap, *all* staff are responsible for SEND achievement.

Schools might question if their disability policy and practice:

- Raises whole-school awareness of the Equality Act and staff responsibilities;
- Identifies who may be disabled under the Act (staff, parents, pupils);
- Identifies pupils who have both SEN and disabilities;
- Takes steps to make reasonable adjustments for all people who may be disabled;
- Examines the impact of related policies and procedures on disability. Are policies adapted in the light of feedback from users?
- Includes an accessibility plan that has involved all staff, external specialists, parents and pupils in writing and evaluating it.

Chapter 4. Inclusion: Access, challenges and barriers

SENCOs need to question how effectively the four 'P's work in their school. How suitable is *place* for all pupils: can either classroom presence or withdrawal be fully justified for each individual? How consistent is whole-school *policy*? How closely do policy and *practice* match? How uniquely personal is *personalisation*?

The Council for Disabled Children (CDC 2008) listed principles of inclusion that schools could use to evaluate themselves. These are:

- A welcome for all disabled pupils;
- Support for families in need;
- Secure staff and pupil relationships;
- Respect for difference;
- Equality of access to all aspects of school life;
- Active participation of children and families in decision-making;
- A proactive approach to identifying and removing barriers;
- Access to information, and to people with empowering attitudes and expertise.

How close is our school to achieving these principles and where are the shortfalls?

Chapter 5. Inclusion for all

The 'for all' movement represents an advanced level of inclusion that is seamless in its overall approach, with SEND learners mixed in and almost invisible within the 'for all' context.

Schools might question:

- How effectively the IDP has been in training up class teachers in SEN?
- How strong is the management grip on whole-school inclusion issues?
- How close is our school to the 2020 vision of appropriate challenge, engagement and ownership for all learners?
- How embedded is the principle of Achievement for All in our school?

Chapter 6. Intervention: Towards a complete package

The success of interventions depends on whether they are reinforced through QFT. Schools could debate:

- How effectively QFT and Wave 2/3 interventions operate as one seamless package;
- How effectively personal plans (IEPs) reflect the complete package, as part of it;
- How well TAs are trained to deliver specific interventions;
- How effectively interventions are evaluated from every perspective: schools, external specialists, parents and learners.

Chapter 7. Learning through personalisation

I believe this to be the biggest challenge of all for most schools, especially at secondary level. The following questions may help all staff to consider how personalisation can support their particular area of teaching, and boost overall achievement:

- How can *all* class and subject teachers be helped to 'find' personalisation from within their pedagogical approaches?
- How are the individual characteristics and personalities of learners with SEND used to advantage, in order to boost achievement?
- How flexible do our school policies need to become in order to accommodate personalised interventions for the few pupils who need them?

Chapter 8. Provision-mapping

Provision-mapping is the key to keeping the whole SEND system together, as well as an efficient problem-solving tool. Debate might focus on:

- How the process of provision-mapping works effectively as a complete cycle; does its evaluation link back to the specific areas highlighted by the audit?
- Do provision-mapping procedures reflect the Code's 'assess, plan, do, review' system?
- Where schools' priorities lie: Improving QFT? More effective interventions?
- How effectively the provision-mapping system coordinates with Code responses and reasonable adjustments;
- How funding is used effectively to produce outcomes, and represent value for money;
- Which model works best for a particular school.

Chapter 9. Reconsidering the school workforce

The SEND system relies on the workforce for its success. How trained up are all members of staff with regard to:

- The vision, aims, objectives and policies of the school?
- Their own roles and responsibilities and how they fit into the big picture?
- How effectively do TAs deliver interventions, and how well are they trained in *specific* as well as generalised intervention needs and procedures?
- How fit for purpose is the school's staffing structure to meet the new SEND challenges?

Where are the gaps and what changes need to be made?

Chapter 10. Developing a SEND-friendly learning environment

For real participation and enhanced achievement to happen most classrooms would benefit from a makeover. It is not a question of working harder. All staff already work as hard as they can. Schools might ask:

- What *changes* in our culture and classroom practice are likely to make the essential differences that count (towards reducing the achievement gap)?
- How effectively do we search for 'iceberg factors' to inform teaching?
- How can learners help to reshape and 'own' their learning environment?
- How well do our classrooms reflect motivation, interaction and engagement *for all*?
- Are our classrooms as fully inclusive and SEND-friendly, as possible?

Chapter 11. Good progress or underachievement?

The shift from SEN processes towards QFT and prevention of SEN in the first place, with high expectations and good progress for all invites debate on:

- How formative (AfL) and summative assessments work effectively together;
- How 'underachievement' is conceptualised and jointly understood amongst all staff;
- How accurately the potential of SEND learners is identified;
- Which vulnerable groups are underachieving against their own potential?
- How does our assessment/evaluation system seek to eradicate underachievement?

Chapter 12. Developing pupil voice and independence

Does developing pupil voice suggest that learners have not previously exercised their voices *influentially* in school? Many haven't. Schools have come a long way since the idea that children should be 'seen but not heard'. Given that schools exist solely for their benefit, the 'pupil voice' quiet revolution is both natural and necessary. Schools might debate whether:

- Pupil voice is really happening in our school; in what ways is it observed?
- How is extended pupil voice influencing change, in QFT? Interventions? Policies?
- How are learners with SEND helped to be part of this development?
- How independent are our learners (including those with SEND) on a scale of 1 to 10?
- Do we have an independence policy? If not, how should we develop one?

Chapter 13. Parents as equal partners

Parents are the most powerful pupil achievement lever schools have, with the potential to exert huge influence over their child's attitudes to education and eventual outcomes. Parents should be at the centre of everything schools and settings do. With regard to SEND, schools might debate the following to support policy:

- How far does our school regard parents as genuinely *equal* partners?
- What use do we make of the information parents have about their SEND child?
- Do we offer parents the opportunities, information and training to be fully engaged?
- How well does our school use the potential of parents to evaluate and improve whole-school policies and systems; for provision-mapping; Code of Practice responses and reasonable adjustments?
- Do our parents *know* they matter? How effectively do we emphasise their importance?

These are questions I think SENCOs and colleagues need to ask about their school's policies and practices, but what about leadership? This is what I think OFSTED will ask of the management team (including SENCOs):

- Have school leaders got a strong grip on their organisation?
- How well have they communicated strategies for raising standards to all stakeholders?
- Are they sufficiently focused on what significantly benefits *all* learners?
- Do they refuse to accept excuses for underachievement?
- Do they do everything possible to compensate for home disadvantage?
- Do leaders challenge staff and pupils to do better?
- Have they established a culture of high aspirations for all learners?

Where are we now?

Education is experiencing a huge turnaround in ethos, culture, policy and practice, perhaps most importantly:

- High expectations and aspirations — education is now regarded as the same journey for all learners — with success (in relative terms) as the ultimate destination: the only difference being that some arrive at their destination earlier than others;
- Learners are now at the heart of *everything* schools and settings do, steering their own progress, supported by person-centred school approaches;
- QFT leads! There has been a shift in focus from intervention as the main solution to SEND achievement. The spotlight now is on ensuring that QFT is the best it can be for all learners, as well as fully inclusive and effective in raising standards;
- The last two chapters of this book summarise the changed context within which SENCOs are most likely to boost success: pupil and parent voices. For too long parents have been the missing link. Establishing equal partnership with all parents is now the priority.

What about children with significant degrees of SEND? As statements become rewritten as EHCPs, these can no longer signal low expectations. Many children with EHCPs *can* and should achieve well. There are further challenges for schools in separating out the needs of pupils receiving 'SEN support'.

There have been many casualties as integration has moved gradually towards inclusion, but without integration we would not have developed inclusion, much less, graduated further towards Achievement for All. Schools now need to hook up with parents and learners to speed up their journey.

A parent has the final word. On Radio 2 the mother of a young person with Down's syndrome explained how an educational psychologist had assessed her daughter as a young child and alerted her not to expect much in attainment *(The Jeremy Vine Show,* 28 April, 2010). This mother then stated that her daughter had obtained five GCSEs at Grades A to C and now has a quality of life on a par with her peers. Exceptional? Maybe. But this is one heart-warming example of how the challenge to break the link between low attainment and learners with SEND *can* deliver. This challenge is not just for schools, but for society.

References

Achievement for All (2009) Guidance for Schools: Characteristics of Effective Inclusive Leadership. National Strategies: DCSF. Available at: http:/ www.essexprimaryheads.co.uk. Last accessed October 2015.

Achievement for All (2014) Impact Report: Raising Aspirations, Access and Achievement. Available at: www.afaeducation.org. Last accessed October 2015.

Association for Achievement and Improvement through Assessment (2015) AAIA. Available at: www.aaia.org.uk. Last accessed October 2015.

B Squared (2015a) Connecting Steps: Sample assessment pages, Core subjects: English, maths and Science. Available at: www.bsquared.co.uk/ConnectingSteps/.../SampleAssessmentPages.aspx. Last accessed October 2015.

B Squared (2015b) Small Steps Summative Assessment. Available at: www.bsquared.co.uk. Last accessed October 2015.

B Squared (2015c) Early Steps Summative Assessment. Available at: www.bsquared/ConnectingSteps/AssessmentAreas/EarlyYears.aspx. Last accessed October 2015.

Barnardo's/Yorkshire and Humberside SEN Regional Partnership (2006) Involving Children and Young People in Meetings and Reviews. (PDF) Available at: www.chimat.org.uk/resource. Last accessed October 2015.

Bercow, J. (2007) Review of Services for Children and Young People (0 to 19) with Speech, Language and Communication Needs. Available at: www.education.gov.uk/publications/.../Bercow-Report.pdf. Last accessed October 2015.

Blanchford, S. (2015) Founder and CEO of AfA: Common-sensing the Code of Practice: Speaker at conference (9.7.15): Centre for Equity in Education: Manchester Metropolitan University. Available at: www.ioe.mmu.ac.uk.

Blatchford, P., Sharples, J. and Webster, R. (2015) Making the Best Use of Teaching Assistants: Guidance Report. Education Endowment Foundation. Available at: www.educationendowmentfoundation.org.uk/.TA guidance Report. Last accessed October 2015.

Brooks, G. (2007) What Works for Pupils with Literacy Difficulties: The Effectiveness of Intervention Schemes (3rd edition). Slough: National Foundation for Educational Research, DCSF. Available at: www.essex.gov.uk. Reference: 00688-2007BKT-EN. Last accessed October 2015.

Brooks, G. (2013) What Works for Children and Young People with Literacy Difficulties: Effectiveness of Intervention Schemes (4th edition), London: Dyslexia/SPLD Trust. Available at: www.interventionsforliteracy.org.uk. Last accessed October 2015.

Burroughs-Lange, S. and Douetil, J. (2006) Evaluation of Reading Recovery in London Schools: Every Child a Reader: 2005-6. Institute of Education, London University. Available: www.ioe.ac.uk. Last accessed October 2015.

Cabinet Office (2005) Improving the Life Chances of Disabled People, Joint report with Dept for Work and Pensions, Department of Health, DfES and Office of Deputy Prime Minister. London. Cabinet Office. Available at: www.webarchive.nationalarchives.gov.uk. Last accessed October 2015.

Carpenter, B., Rose, S., Rawson, H. and Egerton, J. (2011) The Rules of Engagement. Available at: www.complexld.ssatrust.org.uk/uploads/SEN54%20complex%20needs.pdf. Last accessed October 2015.

Cocco, F. (2015) Education: the Pupil Premium had one job — it failed. *Daily Mirror,* 5 February, 2015. Updated 31 March, 2015. Available at: www.mirror.co.uk >News>Ampp3d> Education. Last accessed October 2015.

Council for Disabled Children (2008) Inclusion Policy. Available at: www.councilfordisabledchildren.org.uk/media/59424/Inclusion_Policy.pdf. Last accessed October 2015.

Children's Society (2009) Disability Toolkit. Available at: www.disabilitytoolkit.org.uk. Last accessed October 2015.

DCSF (2007) The Children's Plan: Building Brighter Futures, Nottingham, DCSF. Available at: www.cw.routledge.com/textbooks 9780415485586/data/TheChildrensPlan.pdf. Last accessed October 2015.

DCSF (2008a) Bullying Involving Children with Special Educational Needs and Disabilities: Safe to Learn: Embedding Anti-bullying work in schools. Nottingham: DCSF. Available at: www.norfolk.gov.uk/download/NCC097496. Last accessed October 2015.

DCSF (2008b) The Assessment for Learning Strategy. Nottingham. DCSF. Available at: www.education.gov.uk/publications/.../DCSF-00341-2008.pdf. Last accessed October 2015.

DCSF (2008c) The Inclusion Development Programme Primary/Secondary, Dyslexia and Speech, Language and Communication Needs, Nottingham: DCSF. Available at: www.idponline.org.uk/downloads/ps-dyslexia. Reference 00219-2008 BKT-EN. Last accessed October 2015.

DCSF (2008d) The Inclusion Development Programme, Supporting Children with Speech, Language and Communication Needs. Guidance for Practitioners in the Early Years. Available at: www.idponline.org.uk/downloads/ey-slcn.pdf. Last accessed October 2015.

DCSF (2008e) Every Child a Talker: Guidance for Early Language Lead Practitioners. London: DCSF. Available at: www.webarchive.nationalarchives.gov.uk/.../https:/.../DCSF-00854-2008.pdf. Last accessed October 2015.

DCSF (2008f) The Impact of Parental Involvement on Children's Education. Nottingham: DCSF. Available at: www.education.gov.uk/publications/.../DCSF-Parental_Involvement.pdf. Last accessed October 2015.

DCSF (2009a) Children with Special Educational Needs: an analysis. Available at: www.dera.ioe.ac.uk/9446/1Main.pdf. Last accessed October 2015.

DCSF (2009b) Inclusion Development Programme, Supporting Pupils on the Autism Spectrum DVD and Resource Pack. Nottingham: DCSF. Available at: www.gov.uk/government/uploads/.../00041-2009BKT-EN.pdf. Interactive material also available from the Autism Educational Trust at www.aet.org.uk/. Last accessed October 2015.

DCSF (2009c) Inclusion Development Programme, Supporting Children on the Autism Spectrum: Guidance for Practitioners at the Early Years Foundation Stage. Nottingham: DCSF. Available at: www.gov.uk/government/uploads/.../00040-2009BKT-EN.pdf. Last accessed October 2015.

DCSF (2009d) Your Child, Your Schools, Our Future: Building a 21st Century School System. Nottingham: DCSF. Available at: www.education.gov.uk/publications/.../21st_Century_Schools.pdf. Last accessed October 2015.

DCSF (2009e) Special Educational Needs and Parental Confidence: Report to the Secretary of State on the Lamb Inquiry Review on SEN and Disability Information. Nottingham: DCSF. Available at: www.dyslexiaaction.org.uk/files/dyslexiaaction/_lamb_inquiry.pdf. Last accessed October 2015.

DCSF (2009f) Progression Guidance 2009–10: Improving Data to Raise Attainment and Maximise the Progress of Learners with Special Educational Needs, Learning Difficulties and Disabilities, National Strategies. DCSF. Available at: www.webarchive.nationalarchives.gov.uk/.../8072ae6665f3a3568667710628f6a. Last accessed October 2015.

DCSF (2009g) Gifted and Talented Education: Guidance on Addressing Under-Achievement — Planning a Whole-School Approach. Nottingham: DCSF. Available at: www.education.gov.uk/publications/.../00378-2009BKT-EN.pdf. Last accessed October 2015.

DCSF (2009h) Implementing Every Child a Writer: Primary National Strategies. London: DCSF. Available at: www.dera.ioe.ac.uk/777/7Implementing%20ECaW.Redacted.pdf. Last accessed October 2015.

DCSF (2010a) Inclusion Development Programme Primary and Secondary: Supporting Pupils with Behavioural, Emotional and Social Difficulties, originally a DVD and Resource pack. Nottingham: DCSF. Information Available at: www.idponline.org.uk/downloads/ps-BESD.pdf. Last accessed October 2015.

DCSF (2010b) Inclusion Development Programme: Supporting Children with Social, Emotional and Behavioural Difficulties: Guidance for Practitioners in the Early Years Foundation Stage, Nottingham: DCSF. Available at: www.plymouth.gov.uk/idp_for_behaviour.pdf. Last accessed October 2015.

DCSF (2010c) Breaking the Link between Special Educational Needs and Low Attainment: Everyone's Business, Nottingham: DCSF. Available at: www.education.gov.uk/publications/.../00213-2010DOM-EN.pdf. Last accessed October 2015.

DCSF (2010d) Narrowing the Gaps: Guidance for Literacy Subject Leaders, National Strategies, Nottingham: DCSF. Available at: www.education.gov.uk/publications/.../00083-2010BKT-EN.pdf. Last accessed October 2015.

DCSF/DH (2008) Aiming High for Disabled Children: Transforming Services for Disabled Children and their Families, Nottingham: DCSF. Available at: www.inclusivechoice.com/aiming%20high.pdf. Last accessed October 2015.

DfE (2011a) Leading on Intervention: Strengthening the Quality of Everyday Inclusive Teaching. Originally published by Primary National Strategy. Available at: www.teachfind.com/national-strategies/waves-intervention-model-0. Last accessed October 2015.

DfE (2011b) Evaluating the Impact of Every Child Counts: University of Birmingham posted 4.4.11. Available at: www.birmingham.ac.uk>Newsandevents>News. Last accessed October 2015.

DfE (2012) School Information Regulations: London. DfE. Explanatory memorandum. Available at: www.legislation.gov.uk/uksi/2012/1124/pdfs/uksiem-20121124-en.pdf. Last accessed October 2015.

DfE (2014a) Children and Families Act, London: DfE. Original version. Available at: www.legislation.gov.uk/ukpga2014/6/contents/enacted. The Young Person's Guide Available at: www.gov.uk/.../young-persons-guide-to-the-children- and-families-act. Last accessed October 2015.

DfE (2014b) Equality Act 2010 and Schools: Departmental Advice for School Leaders, School Staff, Governing Bodies and Local Authorities, London: DfE. Available at: www.gov.uk/government/.../equality-act--2010-advice- for-schools. Last accessed October 2015.

DfE (2014c) National Curriculum and Assessment from 2014: Information for Schools, London: DfE. Available at: www.gov.uk/.../NC-assessment-quals- factsheet-Sept-update.pdf. Last accessed October 2015.

DfE (2014d) Performance Descriptors for Use in 2015/16 Statutory Teacher Assessment, London: DfE. Available at: www.gov.uk/.../performance-descriptors-key-stages-1-and-2. Last accessed October 2015.

DfE (2014e) Special Educational Needs and Personal Budgets Regulations, London: DfE. Available at: www.legislation.gov.uk/ukdsi/2014/9780111114056. Last accessed October 2015.

DfE (2014f) Supporting Pupils at School with Medical Conditions: Statutory Guidance for Governing Bodies of Maintained Schools and Proprietors of Academies in England, London: DfE. Available at: www.gov.uk/.../supporting-pupils-at-school-with-medical-conditions. Last accessed October 2015.

DfE (2014g) Preventing and Tackling Bullying: Advice for Headteachers, Staff and Governing Bodies, London: DfE. Available at: www.gov.uk/government/.../Preventing-and-tackling-bullying-advice. Last accessed October 2015.

DfE (2014h) Children with Special Educational Needs: An Analysis: SFR31: Main Text, London: DfE. Available at: www.gov.uk/.../children-with-special-educational-needs-an-analysis. Last accessed October 2015.

DfE (2014i) Performance-P Scale-Attainment Targets for Pupils with Special Educational Needs: A Detailed Guide, London: DfE. Available at: www.gov.uk/.../p-scales-attainment-targets-for-pupils-with-sen (DfE-00484-2014). Last accessed October 2015.

DfE (2014j) SEND Pathfinder Champions: Children and Young People to benefit from SEND Pathfinder: Available at: www.gov.uk/.../children-and-young-people-to-benefit-from-send... Last accessed October 2015.

DfE (2014k) Special Educational Needs and Disability Regulations, London: DfE. Available at: www.legislation.gov.uk/uksi/2014/1530/pdfs/uksi-20141530-en.pdf. Last accessed October 2015.

DfE (2015a) Mental Health and Behaviour in Schools: Departmental Advice for School Staff, London: DfE. Available at: www.gov.uk/government/.../mental-health-and-behaviour-in-schools. Last accessed October 2015.

DfE (2015b) Statistics: Children with Special Educational Needs: London, DfE. Available at: www.gov.uk/.../collections/statistics-special-educational-needs-sen. Last accessed October 2015.

DfE (2015c) Working Together to Safeguard Children: A Guide to Inter-agency Working to safeguard and promote the Welfare of Children. London: DfE. Available at: www.gov.uk/government/.../Working-Together-to-Safeguard-Children.pdf. Last accessed October 2015.

DfE/DH (2015) Special Educational Needs and Disability Code of Practice: 0 to 25 Years: Statutory Guidance for Organisations which work with and support Children and Young People who have Special Educational Needs and Disabilities. London: DfE. Available at: www.gov.uk/government/publications/send-code-of-practice-0-to-25. Last accessed October 2015.

DfEE (2001) Supporting the Target-setting Process: Guidance for Effective Target Setting for Pupils with Special Educational Needs (P Scales), Nottingham: DfEE. Available at: www.education.gov.uk/publications/.../DFEE-0065-2001.pdf. Last accessed October 2015.

DfES (2003a) Every Child Matters, London, DfES. Available at: www.education.gov.uk/publications/eOrdering Download/CM5860.pdf. Last accessed October 2015.

DfES (2003b) Excellence and Enjoyment: A Strategy for Primary Schools, Nottingham: DfES. Available at: www.education.gov.uk/publications/.../dfes-0377-2003PrimaryEd.pdf. Last accessed October 2015.

DfES (2004a) Removing Barriers to Achievement: The Government's Strategy for SEN, London: DfES. Archived but available at: www.advanced-training.org.uk/resources/Universal/removing-barriers.pdf. Last accessed October 2015.

DfES (2004b) Learning and Teaching for Children with Special Educational Needs in the Primary Years, Primary National Strategy, London: DfES. Reference DfES - 03212004 is now archived. Available at: www.webfronter.com/bexley/science/.../SEN-Teaching-and-Learning-DCSF.pdf. Last accessed October 2015.

DfES (2004c) A National Conversation about Personalised Learning, London: DfES. Available at: www.education.gov.uk/publications/.../DfES%200919%20200MIG186.pdf. Last accessed October 2015.

DfES (2005a) Leading on Inclusion, Primary National Strategy, London: DfES. Reference to DfES document 1146355 is now archived. Summary available at: www.thegrid.org.uk>Teaching@Learning>Primary Strategy. Last accessed October 2015.

DfES (2005b) Excellence and Enjoyment: Social and Emotional Aspects of Learning: Guidance: London: DfES. Available at: www.education.gov.uk/publications/.../DFES0110200MIG2122.pdf. Last accessed October 2015.

DfES (2006a) The Deployment and Impact of Support Staff in Schools, London: DfES. Available at: www.dera.ac.uk/23062/1RR776.pdf. Last accessed October 2015.

DfES (2006b) 2020 Vision: Report of the Teaching and Learning in 2020 Review Group, Nottingham: DfES. Available at: www.dera.ioe.ac.uk/6856-DfES-Teaching%20and%20Learning.pdf. Last accessed October 2015.

DfES (2006c) Learning from Every Child A Reader, London: DfES. Available at: www.education.gov.uk/publications/.../lit-intervention-0391806.pdf. Last accessed October 2015.

DfES (2007) Pedagogy and Personalisation, National Strategies, London: DfES. Available at: www.dera.ioe.ac.uk/7585/.../39a74dbb8829067fc3d0a582deb518f5-Redacted.pdf. Last accessed October 2015.

Dowker, A. (2009) What works for Children with Mathematical Difficulties? The Effectiveness of Intervention schemes. DCSF. Available at: www.catchup.org/.../what-works-for-children-with-mathematical-difficulties. Ref. 00086BKT-EN. Last accessed October 2015.

Dunford, J. (2013) A New Direction: Effective Use of the Pupil Premium in Building a Rounded Education for all Young People, Creative Schools Conference, London, 23 October, 2013. Available at: www.anewdirection.org.uk/asset/1115. Last accessed October 2015.

Dyslexia Action (2012) Dyslexia and Literacy Difficulties: Policy and Practice Review: A Consensus Call for Action: Why, What and How: Dyslexia/SPLD Trust. Available at: www.dyslexiaaction.org.uk. Last accessed October 2015.

Dyson, A. (2015) What is problematic about SEN? Transforming the Role of the SENCO, National Award for Special Educational Needs Coordination, Annual Conference, Centre for Equity in Education, Manchester Metropolitan University, 9 July, 2015. Available at: www.ioe.mmu.ac.uk.

Edwards, S. (1999) Speaking and Listening for All, London: David Fulton.

Edwards, S. (2001) Independence for All, Tamworth: NASEN.

Godfrey, W. (2015) Personalised Learning, Transforming the Role of the SENCO, National Award for Special Educational Needs Coordination, Annual Conference, Centre for Equity in Education: Manchester Metropolitan University, 9 July, 2015. Available at: www.ioe.mmu.ac.uk

Harris, A. (2012) Parents Matter: Institute of Education: University of London. Available at: www.almaharris.co.uk/files/parental-engagement.pdf. Last accessed October 2015.

Harris, A. and Goodall, J. (2007) Engaging Parents in Raising Achievement: Do Parents Know they Matter? DCSF. Available at: www.education.gov.uk/publications/.../DCSF-RBW004.pdf. Last accessed October 2015.

Humphrey, N. and Squires, G. (2012) The Impact of AfA on Outcomes for Pupils with Special Educational Needs in English: Lessons for Policy and Practice, Child Health Network Seminar, School of Education, University of Manchester. Available at: www.ihs.manchester.ac.uk/events/pastworkshops/2012/.../presentation.pdf. Last accessed October 2015.

Humphrey, N. and Squires, G. (2013) AfA National Evaluation, London: DfE. Available at: www.gov.uk/government/.../achievement-for-all-national-evaluation. Last accessed October 2015.

Institute of Education, University of London (2011) Every Child a Reader: Annual Report 2009–10. London: European Centre for Reading Recovery. Available at: www.ioe.ac.uk/.../ Every-child-Reader-ECAR-Annual-Report-2009-10. Last accessed October 2015.

Lancashire County Council (2015) Performance Indicators for Valued-added Target Setting (PIVATS), Preston: Lancashire Professional Development Service. Available at: www3.lancashire.gov.uk./corporate/web/?PIVATS/14588. Last accessed October 2015.

Lewis, A., Parsons, S. and Robertson, C. (2007) My School, My Family, My Life: Telling it like it is, Birmingham: Disability Rights Commission, University of Birmingham. Available at: epapers.bham.ac.uk/631/1/Lewis_drc2_2005.pdf. Last accessed October 2015.

Michaelson, M. (2015) Parents and the Law. Transforming the Role of the SENCO. National Award for Special Educational Needs Coordination, Annual Conference, Centre for Equity in Education: Manchester Metropolitan University, 9 July, 2015. Available at: www.ioe.mmu.ac.uk.

Moore, M. (2015) Introduction. Transforming the Role of the SENCO National Award for Special Educational Needs Coordination, Annual Conference, Centre for Equity in Education: Manchester Metropolitan University, 9 July, 2015. Available at: www.ioe.mmu.ac.uk.

National Award for SEN Coordination Learning Outcomes (2014) National College for Teaching and Leadership. Available at: www.gov.uk/.../national-award-for-sen-co-ordination-learning-outcomes. Last accessed October 2015.

National Strategies Teaching Assistant Training Modules. Secondary Intervention. Available at: www.teachfind.com/national-strategies/secondary-intervention-teaching-assistants. Last accessed October 2015.

Oates, T. (2014) Assessment without Levels in depth: Extended version. Cambridge School of Assessment. Available at: www.cambridgeassessment.org.uk/.../assessment-without-levels-extended-version. Last accessed October 2015.

OFSTED (2006) Inclusion: Does it Matter where Pupils are Taught? London: Office for Standards in Education. Available at: www.education.gov.uk/publications/.../HMI-2535.doc.doc. Last accessed October 2015.

OFSTED (2009a) An Evaluation of National Strategy Intervention Programmes: London, OFSTED. Available at: www.dera.ioe.ac.uk/.../An%20evaluation%20of%20National%20Strategy%20intervention%20programmes. Last accessed October 2015.

OFSTED (2009b) Twelve Outstanding Secondary Schools: Excelling against the Odds, London: Office for Standards in Education/Dr. Peter Matthews. Available at: www.lampton.org.uk/wp.../Twelve_outstanding_secondary_schools1.pdf. Last accessed October 2015.

OFSTED (2010) Framework for the Inspection of Maintained Schools in England from September 2009, London: Office for Standards in Education. Available at: www.elc-gel.org/.../the-ofsted-framework-for-school-inspection-jan-2010/. Last accessed October 2015.

OFSTED (2014) Annual Report for 2013/14: Schools. Available at: www.gov.uk/government/collections/ofsted/annual/report-201314. Last accessed October 2015.

Parent Teacher Association (2015) Get the Right School. Available at: www.gettherightschool.co.uk. Last accessed October 2015.

QCA/National Strategies (2008) Assessing Pupil Progress, London: QCA. Available at: www.haslingden.lancsngfl.ac.uk/download/file/app%20PNS.pdf. Last accessed October 2015.

Rose, J. (2006) Independent Review of the Teaching of Early Reading, London: DfES. Available at: www.dera.ioe.ac.uk/5551/2/report.pdf. Last accessed October 2015.

Sacker (2002) 'To explain Social Inequality in Education'. In: Desforges, C. and Abouchaar, A. The Impact of Parental Involvement on Pupil Achievement and Adjustment: A Literature Review, Research Paper number 433, Available at: www.education.gov.uk/publications/eOrderingDownload/RR433.doc. Last accessed October 2015.

Salt, T. (2010) Salt Review: Independent Review of Teacher Supply for Pupils with Severe, Profound and Multiple Learning Difficulties, Nottingham: DCSF. Available at: webarchive.nationalarchives.gov.uk/.../saltreview/.../SaltReportRevisedFinal. Last accessed October 2015.

Spivack, R., Craston, M., Thom, C. and Carr, C. (2014) Special Educational Needs and Disabilities Pathfinder Programme Evaluation Thematic Report: The Education, Health and Care (EHC) Planning Pathway for Families that are new to the SEN System, London, DfE. Available at: www.gov.uk/.../RR326B-EHC_planning_pathway_-_FINAL.pdf. Last accessed October 2015.

Steer, A. (2009) Learning Behaviour: Lessons Learned. A Review of Behaviour Standards and Practices in our Schools. Available at: webarchive.nationalarchives.gov.uk/.../ DCSF-Learning-Behaviour.pdf. Last accessed October 2015.

Szwed, C. (2007) Reconsidering the Role of the Primary Special Educational Needs Coordinator: Policy, Practice and Future Priorities. *British Journal of Special Education*, 34 (2), 96–104. Available at: http://onlinelibrary.wiley.com/doi/10.1111/j.1467-8578.2007.00462.x/abstract. Last accessed October 2015.

TES (2011) Overcoming Barriers Level 3 to Level 4 Maths. Available at: https://www.tes.com/teaching-resource/overcoming-barriers-level-3-to-level-4-maths-6099105. Last accessed October 2015.

Thompson, A. (2015) Special Needs System gets Grade F for Failure, *The Times,* 8 April, 2015. Available at: www.thetimes.co.uk/tto/opinion/columnists/article4404736.ece. Last accessed October 2015.

Training and Development Agency (2009a) National Occupational Standards for Supporting Teaching and Learning, Training and Development Agency (TDA). Available at: www.gov.uk/.../NOS-SUPPORT_for_supporting_teaching_learning. Last accessed October 2015.

Training and Development Agency (2009b) New Training Framework for SENCOs. TDA. Reference Available at: www.nasen.org.uk/.../download.74E8F4BA-8065-4B50-A9F3EAFBB6576. Last accessed October 2015.

Wiltshire Local Authority. Provision-Mapping: A Guide to Developing a Provision Map in the Primary School. Available at: www.wiltshirelocaloffer.org.uk/wp.../provision-mapping-guide.pdf.. Last accessed October 2015.

Worcestershire Health and Care NHS Trust (2013) Every Child a Talker: Evaluation Summary of Worcestershire's ECaT Programme Delivery and Outcomes 2009–2013. Available at: www.languageforlearning.co.uk/images/uploads/5270bd57b58df.pdf Last accessed October 2015.

Useful websites

B Squared Ltd. www.bsquared.co.uk

Catch-up Literacy. www.catchup.org

Emma Rogers Education: Literacy and learning support for schools, networks and local authorities. www.emmarogers.org.uk

Every Child Counts (ECC) programme. www.jobsgopublic.com/vacancy.attachments/61254?source=att

Inclusion Development Programme. www.idponline.org.uk

Leaners First Schools Partnership. www.learnersfirst.net

RAISEonline (Reporting and Analysis for Improvement through School Self-Evaluation). www.raiseonline.org

Reading Recovery International Literacy Centre. www.ilc.ioe.ac.uk

School Pupil Tracker Online (SPTO). www.spto.co.uk/pupiltracker/

SEND Gateway. www.sendgateway.org.uk

Organisations that support SEND Gateway:

Autism Education Trust. www.autismeducationtrust.org.uk
Council for Disabled Children. http://councilfordisabledchildren.org.uk/earlysupport
Excellence Gateway. www.excellencegateway.org.uk
Mind Education. www.minded.org.uk
National Sensory Impairment Partnership. www.natsip.org.uk
The Communication Trust. www.thecommunicationtrust.org.uk
The Dyslexia-spLD Trust. www.thedyslexia-spldtrust.org.uk

Index

Taylor & Francis eBooks

Helping you to choose the right eBooks for your Library

Add Routledge titles to your library's digital collection today. Taylor and Francis ebooks contains over 50,000 titles in the Humanities, Social Sciences, Behavioural Sciences, Built Environment and Law.

Choose from a range of subject packages or create your own!

Benefits for you

- » Free MARC records
- » COUNTER-compliant usage statistics
- » Flexible purchase and pricing options
- » All titles DRM-free.

Benefits for your user

- » Off-site, anytime access via Athens or referring URL
- » Print or copy pages or chapters
- » Full content search
- » Bookmark, highlight and annotate text
- » Access to thousands of pages of quality research at the click of a button.

REQUEST YOUR
FREE
INSTITUTIONAL
TRIAL TODAY

Free Trials Available
We offer free trials to qualifying academic, corporate and government customers.

eCollections – Choose from over 30 subject eCollections, including:

Archaeology	Language Learning
Architecture	Law
Asian Studies	Literature
Business & Management	Media & Communication
Classical Studies	Middle East Studies
Construction	Music
Creative & Media Arts	Philosophy
Criminology & Criminal Justice	Planning
Economics	Politics
Education	Psychology & Mental Health
Energy	Religion
Engineering	Security
English Language & Linguistics	Social Work
Environment & Sustainability	Sociology
Geography	Sport
Health Studies	Theatre & Performance
History	Tourism, Hospitality & Events

For more information, pricing enquiries or to order a free trial, please contact your local sales team:
www.tandfebooks.com/page/sales

Routledge
Taylor & Francis Group

The home of
Routledge books

www.tandfebooks.com